St. Paul's Epistle to theRomans
A Practical Exposition.
(Volume II)

Charles Gore

Alpha Editions

This edition published in 2024

ISBN : 9789362995766

Design and Setting By
Alpha Editions
www.alphaedis.com
Email - info@alphaedis.com

As per information held with us this book is in Public Domain.
This book is a reproduction of an important historical work. Alpha Editions uses the best technology to reproduce historical work in the same manner it was first published to preserve its original nature. Any marks or number seen are left intentionally to preserve its true form.

Contents

PREFACE .... - 1 -

DIVISION IV. CHAPTERS IX-XI. .... - 2 -

DIVISION IV. § 1. CHAPTER IX. 1-13. .... - 8 -

DIVISION IV. § 2. CHAPTER IX. 14-29. .... - 16 -

DIVISION IV. § 3. CHAPTER IX. 30-X. 21. .... - 22 -

DIVISION IV. § 4. CHAPTER XI. 1-12. .... - 29 -

DIVISION IV. § 5[1]. CHAPTER XI. 13-36. .... - 33 -

DIVISION V. CHAPTERS XII-XV. 13. .... - 45 -

DIVISION V. § i. CHAPTER XII. 1-2 .... - 46 -

DIVISION V. § 2. CHAPTER XII. 3-21. .... - 49 -

DIVISION V. § 3. CHAPTER XIII. 1-7. .... - 56 -

DIVISION V. § 4. CHAPTER XIII. 8-10. .... - 61 -

DIVISION V. § 5. CHAPTER XIII. 11-14. .... - 64 -

DIVISION V. § 6. CHAPTER XIV. 1-23. .... - 66 -

DIVISION V. § 7. CHAPTER XV. 1-13. .... - 76 -

DIVISION VI. CHAPTERS XV. 14-XVI. 27. .... - 81 -

DIVISION VI. § 1. CHAPTER XV. 14-33. ....- 82 -

DIVISION VI. § 2. CHAPTER XVI. 1-2. ....- 91 -

DIVISION VI. § 3. CHAPTER XVI. 3-16. ....- 92 -

DIVISION VI. § 4. CHAPTER XVI. 17-20. ....- 96 -

DIVISION VI. § 5. CHAPTER XVI. 21-23. ....- 97 -

DIVISION VI. § 6. CHAPTER XVI. 25-27. ....- 98 -

APPENDED NOTES NOTE A. See vol. i. p. 59. ....- 100 -

PREFACE

There would be no need for a preface to this second volume were it not that a very kindly and careful review of the first volume in The Guardian of May 24 last, requires a word of notice. The reviewer warns me off 'the dialogue system of exegesis.' Now no doubt this principle, like every other, may be abused. 'The Jewish objector' may, as the reviewer complains, be allowed to 'run riot.' Still I cannot doubt that the Jewish objector is a reality of an illuminative kind in the argument of such passages as Romans iii. 1-8, or the great passage (ix-xi), to which the first part of this volume is devoted. Of the other points of detail noticed by the reviewer—which a volume of this kind is not the place to discuss—many are confessedly doubtful, and some unimportant. On most of them I am still disposed to retain my former opinion, but I would, in accordance with my critic's wishes, alter 'the actual life' (vol. i. p. 203) into 'the principle of life,' and (p. 213) instead of saying that the principle of living by dying 'belongs only to a fallen world' say that 'it belongs, as St. Paul views it, though probably not in its ultimate law, to a fallen world.' I agree that in its deepest sense the principle appears to be an ultimate law of all created life of which the conditions are known to us.

C. G.

WESTMINSTER ABBEY,
    Conversion of St. Paul, 1900.

DIVISION IV. CHAPTERS IX-XI.

The theodicy or justification of God for His dealings with the Jews.

St. Paul has concluded his great exposition of the meaning of 'the gospel': that in it is the disclosure of a divine righteousness into which all mankind—Jews and Gentiles on the same level of need and sin—are to be freely admitted by simply believing in Jesus. The believer in Jesus first welcomes the absolute and unmerited forgiveness of his sins, which his redeemer has won for him, and thus acquitted passes into the spiritual strength and joy and fellowship of the new life, the life of the redeemed humanity, lived in Jesus Christ, the second Adam or head of our race. The contemplation of the present moral freedom, and the glorious future prospect, of this catholic body—the elect of God in Jesus Christ—has in the eighth chapter filled the apostle's language with the glow of an enthusiasm almost unparalleled in all the compass of his epistles. And he is intending to pass on to interpret to the representatives of this church of Christ at Rome some of the moral obligations which follow most clearly from the consideration of what their faith really means. This ethical division of the epistle begins with chapter xii. The interval (ix-xi) is occupied with a discussion which is an episode, in the sense that the epistle might be read without it and no feeling of a broken unity would force itself upon us. None the less the discussion not only confronts and silences an obvious objection to St. Paul's teaching, but also brings out ideas about the meaning of the divine election, and the responsibility involved in it, which are vital and necessary for the true understanding of the 'free grace of God.' For these chapters serve really to safeguard the all-important sense of our human responsibility under the rich and unmerited conditions of divine privilege in which we find ourselves.

St. Paul's argument so far has involved an obvious conclusion. God's elect are no longer the Jews in particular. On the contrary, the Jews in bulk have lost their position and become apostates in rejecting the Christ. This result in the first place cuts St. Paul to the heart, for his religious patriotism was peculiarly intense. But in the second place it furnishes an objection in the mouth of the Jew against St. Paul's whole message. For if God had really rejected His chosen people, He had broken His word in so doing. God had pledged Himself to Israel: the Old Testament scriptures were full of passages which might be quoted to this effect. Thus—

'My mercy will I not utterly take from David
'Nor suffer my faithfulness to fail.

'My covenant will I not break,
'Nor alter the thing that is gone out of my lips.
'Once have I sworn by my holiness;
'I will not lie unto David;
'His seed shall endure for ever,
'And his throne as the sun before me.
'It shall be established for ever as the moon,
'And as the faithful witness in the sky[1].'

But according to St. Paul's teaching, had not God 'broken His covenant'? What had become of the 'faithful witness'? To this objection, then, St. Paul sets himself to reply. The chapters we are now to consider may be best represented as an animated defence of his teaching directed toward a Jew who pleads this objection. St. Paul, no doubt, had heard too much of it since he began to preach the gospel, and had felt it too deeply in his own mind in the earlier days, when the word of Jesus was as a goad against which he was kicking, for it to be possible for him to pass it by. And his defence—his 'theodicy' or justification of God—is in brief this: God never committed Himself or tied Himself to Israel physically understood. He always kept hanging over their heads declarations of His own freedom in choosing His instruments, and warnings of possible rejection, such as ought to have prevented their resting satisfied with merely having 'Abraham to their father' (ix). And if the question be asked: Why has Israel been rejected? The answer is: That so far as actual Israel has fallen out of the elect body, it is because they refused to exhibit the correspondence of faith (x); but also Israel, as such, has not been rejected; for, as of old, so now there is a faithful remnant. Nor again is the partial alienation of Israel which has occurred final. God is simply waiting for their recovery of faith, to restore them to their ancient and inalienable position of election. Meanwhile He uses their temporary alienation as the opportunity of the Gentiles, who in their turn can only retain their newly won position by maintaining the correspondence of faith with the purposes of God, and who also wait for their fulfilment and the perfecting of their joy upon the recovery of Israel as a body. Thus through all stages of election and rejection—by both methods of mercy and of judgement—God, in His inscrutable wisdom, works steadily for the opportunity of showing His mercy upon all men.

When we have a brief analysis of the argument of these chapters under our eyes, we may well rub them in astonishment, and look again, and ask why, in the reaction against Calvinism[2], we had come (to put it frankly) to dislike these chapters so much. We know that as a fact these chapters have been taken as a stronghold of the Calvinistic position by both its friends and foes. They have come to constitute in modern literature a sort of reproach upon Christianity[3], just on the ground on which the best Christian conscience of our time is most sensitive. Many of us would have to admit that we have shrunk from these chapters as we have heard them read, and probably avoided them in our own reading. We have shrunk from the sound of the words—'the children being not yet born, neither having done anything good or bad, that the purpose of God according to election might stand, not of works but of him that calleth'—'Jacob have I loved, and Esau have I hated'—'Whom he will he hardeneth'—'Hath not the potter power over the clay.' Yet these texts, with their arbitrary, unfair and narrow sound, appear as steps in an argument which has for its conclusion the most universal conception possible of the purpose of the divine love. 'God shut up all unto disobedience, that he might have mercy upon all.' The conclusion of the argument is so unmistakable, and so plain against any Calvinistic attribution to God of a narrow and arbitrary favouritism, that there must have been some great mistake in our understanding of its main point and drift. It is worth while then to indicate at starting where the error has lain.

1. It has been in part owing to our mistaken habit of taking isolated 'texts' out of their connexion, as if they were detached aphorisms. Now St. John, in his meditative method, does very generally round off a fundamental Christian truth into an aphorism which really admits of being detached and quoted apart from its context. And no doubt there are in St. Paul detachable texts. But on the whole St. Paul, least of all men, admits of being judged by detached fragments. His thought is always in process. It looks before and after. He is seriously wronged by the mere fact of his epistles being divided into separate verses, and sometimes arbitrary chapters, as in the Authorized Version. Thus in the case of these three chapters, the common mistake as to the meaning of particular phrases could hardly have arisen if the argument had been kept in mind as a whole, and especially its conclusion as to the universal purpose of divine love—'to have mercy upon all.'

2. For, among other things, the true meaning of 'election' in these chapters would then have been apparent. St. Paul has been popularly misunderstood to be referring to God's 'election' of some individual men to salvation in heaven, and His abandonment of the rest to hell. Whereas the argument as a whole and its conclusion make it quite certain that what he is speaking of is the election of men in nations or churches (only subordinately of individuals)[4] to a position of special spiritual privilege and responsibility in this world, such as the Jews had formerly occupied, and the Christians were occupying now—an election to be the people of God, and bear His name in the face of the world—the sort of election which carries with it a great joy and a special opportunity, but not by any means a certainty of final

personal acceptableness to God, apart from moral faithfulness. Apart from such faithfulness the 'children of the kingdom shall be cast into the outer darkness,' and the highest shall be put lowest, while the lowest are raised highest.

3. Another cause of misunderstanding has been forgetfulness of the point of view of the opponent with whom St. Paul is arguing. In modern times assertions of divine absoluteness, like St. Paul's, have been made by teachers who were refusing to recognize any such freedom of the will in the individual human being—any such power to control his own personal destiny—as seems to our common sense to be involved in moral responsibility in any real sense. St. Paul has therefore been supposed, like these more recent teachers, to be asserting divine absoluteness, or the unrestricted freedom of divine choice, as against human freedom, or in such a way as to destroy the idea of moral responsibility. But in fact St. Paul is vindicating moral responsibility. His opponent is the Jew, who holds that God had so tied His hands and lost His liberty in choosing Israel once for all for His elect people, that every child of Abraham can at all times claim the privileges of his election for no other reason than because of his genealogy. Such a doctrine of election does indeed destroy all real moral responsibility in the subject of it, and all freedom of moral choice in God. St. Paul, on the other hand, asserts that God remains free and absolute to elect and to reject, irrespective of all questions of race, where He will and as He will. The absolute reason of God's selections, the reason why certain races and individuals are chosen for special privileges and as special instruments of the divine purpose, lies in a region into which we cannot penetrate. But because God has shown us His moral character and requirement, we can know how, and how only, we may hope to retain any position which God has given us; it is by exhibiting moral correspondence with His purpose—that is faith—or malleability under His hand.

This is a doctrine then which lays upon 'the elect,' at any particular moment, the moral responsibility of correspondence with a divine purpose. In a word, St. Paul asserts divine sovereignty in such a sense as vindicates instead of destroying moral responsibility, while his opponent is claiming for Israel a sort of freedom from being interfered with, which would really destroy their moral responsibility altogether. Thus, as has already been pointed out[5], nothing can well be more important than to keep clearly in mind, here as elsewhere, with whom St. Paul is arguing.

4. It is worth while remarking, before we apply ourselves to St. Paul's argument in detail, that it is essentially 'apologetic': it is a justification of God in view of certain felt difficulties: and it is an argument ad hominem, that is an argument with certain people on their own assumptions, the sort of argument which takes the form of saying, 'you at least have no right on

your own principles to urge such and such difficulties.' Now we are bound to recognize how very important at all periods this ad hominem appeal is: how very important it is to get men to see what their own principles really involve. A great part of the evil of the world comes through people not thinking out what they really mean and believe. But on the other hand, this sort of argument, which proceeds upon a certain set of assumptions, has often a merely temporary force, and carries with it an accompanying danger. When the state of mind contemplated becomes a matter of history, the argument based on its assumption has lost its power. In view of a quite different set of assumptions it may become even misleading. For example, Bishop Butler argued for the truths of natural and revealed religion, on the analogy of the facts of nature and on the assumption of a divine author of nature, thus—If, as you admit, God made nature, and yet nature is shown to contain such and such facts or processes, how can you argue against the divine authorship of natural religion and revelation on the ground that it attributes to God similar facts and processes? This was a very effective argument so long as men did treat the doctrine of God having created the world as a matter of course. But when 'agnosticism' arose—when men ceased to discover in nature any decisive argument for God or against God, and professed only an inability to draw any conclusion at all, Butler's argument had lost its force, and the difficulties in nature and religion to which he called attention could even be used against ascribing a divine authorship to either. Apologetic arguments are always liable to this peril. Thus St. Paul's arguments, based on an unhesitating belief that the Old Testament contained really the words of God, that what they asserted about God was certainly true, and that God was certainly just and the standard of justice, may have an effect very contrary to his intention when they are applied to people who feel no such certainties. St. Paul may seem to be making the difficulties of believing in the Bible only more obvious, by calling attention to its 'harsh and unedifying' elements.

But this unfortunate result of most 'apologies' is, at least in the case of St. Paul and Bishop Butler, only superficial. If the apologetic argument is really deep, it retains, if not exactly its original value, yet a value not the less real. Butler's indications of the profound analogy which holds between the doctrines of religion and the facts of nature, can never be out of place or lose force. Still less can men ever cease to learn the deepest lessons from his temper of mind and method. And that it is so with St. Paul's apology—that it contains the profoundest and most abiding lessons about the responsibility and danger of all elect bodies and individuals—will appear plainly enough in what follows, now that we are in a position to approach his argument in detail.

[1] Ps. lxxxix. 33-7.

[2] By this phrase is commonly meant the doctrine that God created some men absolutely and irresistibly predestined to eternal life and joy, and created the rest of mankind absolutely and hopelessly abandoned to eternal misery.

[3] Matthew Arnold, St. Paul and Protestantism (Smith, Elder, 1870), p. 99, admits that St. Paul 'falls into Calvinism,' but patronizingly excuses him on the ground that this Calvinism is with him secondary, or even less than secondary.

[4] Of course the election of the nation or the church is felt, especially in the New Testament, or whenever in the Old Testament individuality is fully realized, to involve the election of each of the persons composing the nation or the church. But still their election is a challenge to their faith, and no guarantee of ultimate salvation. St. Paul is left praying and suffering 'for the elect's sake that they also may obtain the salvation ... with eternal glory' (2 Tim. ii. 10). The elect have to 'make their calling and election sure' (2 Peter i. 10). It should, however, be noticed that election may be, and in the Gospels is, used to describe the final selection of those who are proved worthy of the 'marriage supper of the Lamb.' (Matt. xxii. 14.)

[5] Vol. i. pp. 114 f.

DIVISION IV. § 1. CHAPTER IX. 1-13.

The present rejection of Israelites no breach of a divine promise.

St. Paul has finished his glowing description of the position and prospects of the elect people of God. And then, by contrast, the misery of the outcast people once called elect—his own people—wrings his heart with pain. The very idea that in his new enthusiasm for the catholic church he can be supposed to be forgetting those who are of his own flesh and blood, stirs him to a profound protest. He solemnly asseverates that the pain which Israel's rejection causes him is acute and continuous. He has caught himself at the point of praying to be himself an outcast from Christ, if so be he could bring the people of his own kindred and blood into the Church. For who indeed could seem to have so good a title to be there? They are the Israelites—that is God's own people: the eye of God was so specially upon this race that He redeemed it and made it His own son[1]: to them was vouchsafed the shining of His continual presence in the tabernacle[2]: to them, in the persons of the patriarchs and of Moses, God gave special covenants, that is to say, pledged His word to them in an unmistakable manner and repeatedly that He should be their God and they should be His people: thus in pursuance of a divine purpose they were brought under the education of the divinely given law and ritual worship: and all this with direct and repeated promises of a more glorious position in the future to be brought about by the divine king, the Christ who was to be. To them finally belongs all the sanctity which can attach to a people from having numbered among its members the holy ones of God: for of this race were the patriarchs, the friends of God; and of this race, so far as human birth is concerned, came in fact the Christ who, born a Jew, is sovereign of the universe and ever blessed God. Surely then, St. Paul implies, that this race, now that the Christ they were expecting is at last come, now that the goal of all God's dealings with them is at last reached, should have fallen outside the circle of His people and be no longer sharers in the sonship or the election, would seem a result too monstrous to contemplate. The contrast between what they were and were intended for, and what in present appearance they are, is indeed appalling.

Yet the natural conclusion for the Jew to draw, which at this point flashes into St. Paul's mind, the conclusion that God has proved unfaithful, is not the true one. No: God's word, God's promise, has not broken down. For, if the facts are looked at, it appears quite plainly that the Israel of God was never simply the Israel of physical descent, nor the children of Abraham simply his physical seed. Plainly not. For Isaac and Ishmael were equally

Abraham's seed, physically considered, but for the purpose of God the promise is given only to the family of the younger son, Isaac (Gen. xxi. 12), who moreover was born, not in the mere natural order, but under circumstances of special divine promise and intervention (Gen. xviii. 10). And if in this case it be said that the younger son Isaac was the only son of Sarah, the wife and free woman, and therefore had a natural prerogative over Ishmael, yet the same inscrutable principle of selection is apparent in the next generation, in a case where there is no possible inequality of natural claim—in the case of the two sons born simultaneously to Isaac of the same mother. Prior to their birth, and prior therefore to any possible merit or demerit on their own part—so that God's absolute freedom of choice should appear quite conspicuously—the younger Jacob was deliberately preferred over the elder Esau (Gen. xxv. 23). And in fact this race of Esau, this Edom—though they were Israelites after the flesh—appear in history as something much worse than merely secondary to the true Israel; for God speaks by Malachi and declares that, whereas Israel is His beloved son, Esau, that is Edom, He has 'hated' (Mal. i. 3). No Israelite therefore who reads his scriptures (St. Paul would conclude) ought to have failed to perceive an inscrutable element in God's choice of his chosen people. He ought not to have felt in his own case, any more than in that of the first children of Abraham or Isaac, that he could be sure of membership in the people of God merely because of his physical descent.

I say the truth in Christ, I lie not, my conscience bearing witness with me in the Holy Ghost, that I have great sorrow and unceasing pain in my heart. For I could wish[3] that I myself were anathema from Christ for my brethren's sake, my kinsmen according to the flesh: who are Israelites; whose is the adoption, and the glory, and the covenants, and the giving of the law, and the service of God, and the promises; whose are the fathers, and of whom is Christ as concerning the flesh, who is over all, God blessed for ever. Amen. But it is not as though the word of God hath come to nought. For they are not all Israel, which are of Israel: neither, because they are Abraham's seed, are they all children: but, In Isaac shall thy seed be called. That is, it is not the children of the flesh that are children of God; but the children of the promise are reckoned for a seed. For this is a word of promise, According to this season will I come, and Sarah shall have a son. And not only so; but Rebecca also having conceived by one, even by our father Isaac—for the children being not yet born, neither having done anything good or bad, that the purpose of God according to election might stand, not of works, but of him that calleth, it was said unto her, The elder shall serve the younger. Even as it is written, Jacob I loved, but Esau I hated.

1. St. Paul's earnest asseveration is very noticeable in form. It shows so much of his instinctive inward life. He lives 'in Christ,' who is light as well as life[4], and to speak the truth is the very atmosphere of this new life[5]. As it comes natural to many people to say 'upon my word as a gentleman,' it comes natural to St. Paul to say, 'speaking as in Christ, who is the light.' And his natural conscience—that is the faculty of passing judgement on one's own actions, which in St. Paul's case bears witness to the truth of what he says by passing no censure on him—that too does not act of itself merely, but in the Spirit of the new life, the Holy Spirit of Christ, which inspires and ratifies the moral judgement, otherwise so liable to be degraded or perverted or silenced: his conscience bears witness with his word in the Holy Ghost. Here, then, is the whole secret of Christian truthfulness. The Christian is truthful because he lives and speaks in God, in Christ, in the Spirit.

As to St. Paul's half-expressed prayer ('I was praying,' he says, i.e. 'I caught myself praying'), it resembles that of Moses for his rebellious people[6]. 'And now, O Lord, if thou wilt forgive their sin—; and if not, blot me, I pray thee, out of thy book which thou hast written.' But St. Paul's instinctive desire is not apparently like that of Moses, to perish with his people rather than be saved without them; but to offer himself for rejection with a view to their salvation. The prayer is, as St. Paul implies, an impossible prayer, but it expresses, as hardly anything else could, the intensity of his feeling. And such intensity of feeling was natural to the deep religious patriotism of a Jew.

We may illustrate St. Paul's feeling by comparing a fine expression of a more commonplace sorrow over the ruin of Israel from a period after the destruction of Jerusalem[7]. 'Now therefore I will speak; touching man in general, thou knowest best; but touching thy people will I speak, for whose sake I am sorry; and for thine inheritance, for whose cause I mourn; and for Israel, for whom I am heavy; and for the seed of Jacob, for whose sake I am troubled.' 'Thou seest that our sanctuary is laid waste, our altar broken down, our temple destroyed; our psaltery is brought low, our song is put to silence, our rejoicing is at an end; the light of our candlestick is put out, the ark of our covenant is spoiled, our holy things are defiled, and the name that is called upon us is profaned; our freemen are despitefully treated, our priests are burnt, our Levites are gone into captivity, our virgins are defiled, and our wives ravished; our righteous men carried away, our little ones betrayed, our young men are brought into bondage, and our strong men are become weak; and, what is more than all, the seal of Sion—for she hath now lost the seal of her honour, and is delivered into the hands of them that hate us.'

2. As we read St. Paul's enumeration of the glories of Israel, it is of course obvious for us to pursue the line of thought taught us elsewhere by St. Paul, and in the Epistle to the Hebrews; and to recognize how each element of the 'glory,' which belonged once to the Jewish 'ministration of condemnation,' belongs in deeper and fuller measure to the Christian 'ministration of the Spirit[8].' Ours is the vocation of the chosen people; ours is the sonship to God; and the perpetual presence; and the security of divine covenant; ours is the divine law, and with it, what is much better, the Spirit for its accomplishment; ours is the corporate worship in spirit and in truth, the Church's eucharist; for us, too, are promises which the realization of those of the first covenant has made 'more sure'; ours finally is the communion of the saints from Abraham onward into the body of Christ. And in proportion therefore to the greatness of our privileges, even as compared with those of the older covenant, is the greatness of our responsibility; 'For I would not, brethren, have you ignorant[9],' St. Paul would say; he would not have us fail to profit by the warnings of old days. And another voice warns us 'Of how much sorer punishment shall he be thought worthy, who hath trodden under foot the Son of God, and hath counted the blood of the covenant, wherewith he was sanctified, an unholy thing, and hath done despite unto the Spirit of grace[10].'

3. There has been amongst critics, since Erasmus, much controversy over the clause, 'who is over all, God blessed for ever.' There is no doubt that it is translated most naturally, and most agreeably to the balance and movement of the sentence, if we attribute it to Christ, as above. But many critics, including some who were orthodox, have stumbled at the idea of St. Paul speaking of Christ straight out as 'over all, God blessed for ever.' Generally no doubt 'God' is used by St. Paul as a proper name of the Father. But Christ is continually recognized as possessing strictly divine attributes, and exercising strictly divine functions; and in all St. Paul's epistles, beginning with his earliest to the Thessalonians, He is God's Son, His own or proper Son[11]. His blood, as shed for our ransoming, is God's own blood, or (possibly) the blood of one who is 'His own'[12]. He subsisted eternally in the form, or essential attributes, of God, and in possession of equality with Him; and He possesses now, as glorified in humanity, the divine name of universal sovereignty, the object of universal worship[13]. Therefore He is in the strictest sense divine; and whatever or, I should say, whoever is essentially divine and proper to the being of God, can rightly be called God. For, indeed, there is nothing in the strict sense divine but God Himself. It was then merely a question of time when Christians would become sufficiently familiar with the new revelation of the threefold name to apply the word God to the Son and the Spirit as naturally as to the Father. And there is nothing really to surprise us in St. Paul here applying it to Christ[14]: nothing certainly to warrant us in doing violence

to the sentence, in order to obviate the conclusion that he did so, by putting a full stop after 'flesh,' and then supposing an abrupt exclamation 'He who is over all is God blessed for ever[15]!'

Let it be recognized, then, that St. Paul here plainly speaks of Christ as 'over all,' i.e. in His glorified manhood, and also as 'God blessed for ever'— that is, as the one proper and eternal object of human praise; and that he speaks of Him again elsewhere[16], as 'our great God and Saviour.' It was only because He was essentially and eternally 'God' that He could, in our manhood and as the reward of His human obedience, be exalted to divine sovereignty and be 'over all.'

4. In the rest of the section St. Paul is arguing with a Jew, who makes the claim that because of the divine covenant God is bound to the Israelites, and to all Israelites for ever. 'We have Abraham to our father,' and that is enough[17]. The higher prophetic spirit of the Old Testament had already realized that God's election of Israel was a challenge to her to prove herself worthy of an undeserved privilege[18], and that, though a faithful remnant would never fail, yet unfaithfulness in the bulk of the nation would bring destruction upon them and loss of God's favour[19]. The prophetic spirit had realized also that God's servant Israel was not 'called' for his own selfish honour's sake, but was entrusted with a divine ministry to fulfil for all the nations of the earth[20]. It is to this higher sense of what Israel's position meant, and the perils it involved, that John the Baptist and our Lord Himself had sought to recall the Jews. They must not 'think to say within themselves, They had Abraham for their Father; for God was able of the stones to raise up children unto Abraham.' For 'many should come from the east and the west, and sit down with Abraham, and Isaac, and Jacob, in the kingdom of God, and the sons of the kingdom should be cast into the outer darkness[21].' But it is evident that this higher meaning of the doctrine of election had been forgotten by contemporary Judaism, and they would not be recalled to it. They refused to contemplate the spiritual risk of missing their vocation, or the universal purpose for which it was given. They chose to think that Israel, i.e. the actual Israelites in bulk, must remain God's elect; that the Christ, when He came, must come to exalt their race and nation: that they were bound to inherit the blessings of the world to come: that the divine government of the world existed for their sakes[22].

St. Paul, then, is here intending to vindicate the real meaning of election, in the sense in which it is bound up with the ethical character of God and carries with it a deepened feeling of responsibility in those who are the subjects of it. But his argument is directed, first of all, to one point only— to bringing the eyes of the Jews straight up to their own scriptures, and forcing them to see that they do not justify the idea of election purely by race. It is not all of a certain seed, but only part of it, that is chosen. There is nothing to hinder a great part of the race again becoming as Ishmael or as Edom by the side of Israel. Ultimately, no doubt, there are two points to be proved. First, that God's method of choosing an elect body to be His people in the world is inscrutable, so that we cannot produce or determine His election by any calculation, or by any real or supposed merits, of ours; secondly, that though we cannot create our vocation, we can retain it by moral correspondence or faith, and by that only. But at present it is only the first point that is insisted upon—the absolute, inscrutable element in the divine choice. And that, we should notice, is a fact not merely of scriptural evidence but of common experience. Men are born to higher and lower positions of privilege and opportunity. They are born Jacobs or Esaus, in respect of moral, intellectual, religious, or physical endowment—with ten talents, or five, or two, or one; and God does not often give us so much as a glimpse of the reason why. All He does make clear to us is that the determination of human vocations, higher or lower, is in wiser hands than ours.

It is of course evident, as has already been said, that what St. Paul is speaking about is the election of men, and specially races or nations of men, to a position of spiritual privilege in this world. We know now, better than the Jews of the Old Covenant could know it, that behind all the apparent injustices and inequalities of this world lies the rectifying equity of God. St. Peter had come to believe that the divine mercy had rectified in the world beyond death the apparently rough and heavy handed judgement upon the rejected mass of mankind in the time of the Flood. That physical catastrophe at least was an instrument of mercy in disguise[23]. St. Paul believed the same about all God's rejections, as well as elections, in this world. They served one universal purpose: 'That he might have mercy upon all[24].' But all the same here and now in this world God does work by means of enormous inequalities. There are Jacobs whom He plainly loves, upon whom He showers all His richest blessings, and Esaus whom, to judge from present evidence, we should say He hates—whom He sets to live in hardest and most cramping surroundings. And no man can determine which lot he shall enjoy. That lies in the inscrutable selectiveness of God.

That there is no question at all about the eternal welfare of the individual Esau's soul—that the question is simply of the comparative status of Israel and Edom in this world—appears plainly in the passage of Malachi, which St. Paul quotes. And we must notice how unexpected an application St. Paul gives to this passage in a direction most unfamiliar to Jewish thought. For Edom was to the Jew the very type of all that was most hateful. He anticipated for the Edomites God's worst vengeance, as for Israel God's best blessings. But St. Paul forces him to think—Why should he assume that he will be better off than Edom? Edom was once physically on Israel's level, or his superior in claim, when their first fathers were but just born infants. But God chose one and not the other. He may exercise the like unscrutable selectiveness upon the seed of Israel to-day. And Edom did not remain in a merely secondary position. He sank to be a byword for all that is most hateful to God. Be warned, St. Paul would say, it may be that 'with change of name the tale is told of thee[25].'

[1] Exod. iv. 23; Hos. xi. 1.

[2] Exod. xvi. 10.

[3] Or 'pray' (marg.) literally 'I was praying.'

[4] Cf. Eph. v. 8-14.

[5] Cf. Col. iii. 9.

[6] Exod. xxxii. 32.

[7] 2 Esdr. viii. 15-16, x. 21-23. The latter passage is not spoken to God, but by one Jew to another.

[8] 2 Cor. iii. 8.

[9] See 1 Cor. x. 1-13.

[10] Heb. x. 29.

[11] 1 Thess. i. 10; Rom. viii. 3.

[12] Acts xx. 28.

[13] Phil. ii. 6-11.

[14] Without the article which makes it a proper name of the Father.

[15] R. V. margin[2]. It does further violence to the Greek to translate as R. V. margin[1], 'He who is God over all is (be) blessed for ever.' I have nothing to add on the matter to S. and H. in loc., especially p. 236.

[16] Tit. ii. 13. This is probably the right rendering.

[17] St. Matt. iii. 9.

[18] Great stress was laid by the prophets on the absence of any original merit or power in Israel, which caused the divine election; see Ezek. xvi, Deut. xxvi. 5.

[19] See especially Amos ix. 7-10: 'Are ye not as the children of the Ethiopians unto me, O children of Israel? saith the Lord. Have not I brought up Israel out of the land of Egypt, and the Philistines from Caphtor, and the Syrians from Kir? Behold, the eyes of the Lord God are

upon the sinful kingdom, and I will destroy it from off the face of the earth; saving that I will not utterly destroy the house of Jacob, saith the Lord. For, lo, I will command, and I will sift the house of Israel among all the nations, like as corn is sifted in a sieve, yet shall not the least grain fall upon the earth. All the sinners of my people shall die by the sword, which say, The evil shall not overtake nor prevent us.'

[20] Gen. xii. 3; Isa. lxvi. 18; Zech. viii. 23, &c.

[21] Matt. viii. 11, 12.

[22] In Weber's Jüdische Theologie (Leipzig, 1897, formerly called System der Altsynagog. Palästin. Theol. or Die Lehre des Talmud), pp. 51 ff, there are striking illustrations from the Talmud of this fixed tendency of thought among the Jews. Thus 'there exists no clearer proof of the Talmudic conviction of the absolutely holy character of Israel than that in all the places of Scripture in which Israel is reproved and has evil attributed to it, the expression, "the haters of Israel," is substituted for Israel.' 'We read: Isaiah was punished, because he called Israel a people of unclean lips,' &c. Cf. S. and H., p. 249, and my Ephesians, p. 261.

[23] 1 Pet. iv. 6. 'The gospel was preached to' these 'dead men that they might be judged according to men in the flesh,' i.e. by perishing in the flood, 'but live according to God in the spirit,' i.e. through our Lord's preaching in Hades. There is, I think, so far, no ambiguity about this passage.

[24] Not, however, without regard to man's will to respond to the divine offer, see later, p. 82 ff.

[25] Mal. i. 2, 3. 'Was not Esau Jacob's brother? saith the Lord: yet I loved Jacob; but Esau I hated, and made his mountains a desolation, and gave his heritage to the jackals of the wilderness. Whereas Edom saith, We are beaten down, but we will return,' &c. This passage (1) plainly refers to Esau as meaning Edom, the people; (2) describes not the original lot of Esau, which was secondary indeed, but highly blessed (Gen. xxvii. 39, 40); but the ultimate lot of Esau when he had misused his original endowment in violence and cruelty.

DIVISION IV. § 2. CHAPTER IX. 14-29.

God's liberty in showing mercy and judgement always retained and asserted.

But the obvious reply of the Jewish objector to St. Paul's assertion of the absolute and apparently arbitrary freedom of God's election is that it is unfair. It convicts God of unrighteousness. To this objection (ver. 14), which St. Paul deprecates with horror, he replies not by any large consideration of divine justice, but still by keeping the Jew to his own scriptures. The God revealed in scripture must be to the objector still the just God. He cannot call God unjust if His method as it now appears is that to which He called attention long ago. Look back, then, at the past records. Did God disclose Himself as bound to show mercy on Moses the Israelite, or to harden and judicially condemn Pharaoh the Egyptian? No, He declares to Moses His unrestricted freedom to exhibit His compassion on whom He will (Exod. xxxiii. 19). Men cannot by any choice or efforts of their own produce an exhibition of divine favour such as was shown to Moses the leader of Israel: the absolute initiative must come from God, and in taking that initiative He declares Himself absolutely free. In the same way God implicitly asserts His sovereign freedom when He brings Pharaoh out upon the stage of history as an example of the way in which He hardens men's hearts with a hardening which is the prelude to overthrow, that men all over the world may see and tremble at the divine power. It is not because Pharaoh is an Egyptian that he is hardened. He is hardened, as Moses has compassion shown him, simply because it is the will of God so to do in his case.

But the objector comes forward again (ver. 19): 'If this is the arbitrary method of God—if we are simply powerless puppets in the hands of an absolute and arbitrary will, to be saved or be destroyed—at any rate He has no reason to complain of us. If all the power is His, so is the responsibility.' Now St. Paul has it in his hand to show that there remains to man a very real power to retain his position, and consequently a very real responsibility and room for being blamed or praised: for if we cannot create our vocation, we can and we are required to correspond with it in a reverent and docile faith; and it was exactly here that the Jews had failed, in spite of all their prophets had taught them. But he keeps back this answer awhile, because he finds the attitude of such an objector toward God in itself so reprehensible. Such an one has not given consideration to what the relation of man to God really is—the creature to the creator. His critical, complaining attitude is nothing better than foolish.

Thus he takes his antagonist back upon the old prophetic metaphor of the potter and his clay, with which Isaiah and Jeremiah had rebuked the arrogance and impatience of men long ago: 'Shall the thing framed say of him that framed it, He hath no understanding; and shall the clay say to him that fashioneth it, What makest thou[1]?' He follows, however, most closely upon the later writer of the Book of Wisdom: 'For a potter, kneading soft earth, laboriously mouldeth each several vessel for our service: nay, out of the same clay doth fashion both the vessels that minister to clean uses, and those of a contrary sort. All in like manner; but what shall be the use of each vessel of either sort, the craftsman himself is the judge[2].' The thought was often in St. Paul's mind of the inequality of lots in the world and the Church. There are more and less honourable limbs in the body politic: there are vessels for honourable and vessels for dishonourable purposes in the great social economy[3]. So it is with the races of men. They are all of one blood—of the one lump. But some have high and others low vocations, and the right to determine of what sort the lot shall be in each case lies absolutely with the Divine Potter. It is childish to dispute His title. And not only so: when the potter, whom Jeremiah was ordered to observe, found a vessel he was making marred under his hand, 'he made it again another vessel, as seemed good to the potter to make it[4].' Accordingly, when the chosen material (i.e. the Jews) would not mould to the high purpose for which the Potter was fashioning it, who shall complain if He diverted it to lower uses or threw it away to destruction, and produced out of His stores other vessels which He had already prepared and destined for glorious functions (that is to say, the Gentile Christians)? But the case is even stronger than this. Who indeed shall complain if, when the vessels originally destined for the higher uses prove fit for nothing but destruction, the Divine Potter—though willing, now as in the case of Pharaoh, to let His wrath fall and to manifest His power—yet shows almost unlimited forbearance with them (as in fact God did with the Jews); and when at last He does let His wrath fall, only does so in order to manifest anew the resourcefulness of His mercy[5] upon a new and larger Israel, gathered not from among the Jews only, but from among all nations, to be the object of His compassionate regard?

Indeed, the prophet Hosea (ii. 23, i. 10) foresaw this choice of a yet unrecognized people to be God's people. Isaiah again (x. 22) anticipated no more than a remnant surviving of all the multitudes of Israel, because of the sharpness and conclusiveness of the divine judgement upon them. And (i. 9) it is only to the compassion of God that he attributes their exemption by means of the faithful remnant from entire annihilation, like that of the Cities of the Plain.

What shall we say then? Is there unrighteousness with God? God forbid. For he saith to Moses, I will have mercy on whom I have mercy, and I will have compassion on whom I have compassion. So then it is not of him that willeth, nor of him that runneth, but of God that hath mercy. For the scripture saith unto Pharaoh, For this very purpose did I raise thee up, that I might shew in thee my power, and that my name might be published abroad in all the earth. So then he hath mercy on whom he will, and whom he will he hardeneth.

Thou wilt say then unto me, Why doth he still find fault? For who withstandeth his will? Nay but, O man, who art thou that repliest against God? Shall the thing formed say to him that formed it, Why didst thou make me thus? Or hath not the potter a right over the clay, from the same lump to make one part a vessel unto honour, and another unto dishonour? What if God, willing to shew his wrath, and to make his power known, endured with much longsuffering vessels of wrath fitted unto destruction: and that he might make known the riches of his glory upon vessels of mercy, which he afore prepared unto glory, even us, whom he also called, not from the Jews only, but also from the Gentiles? As he saith also in Hosea,

I will call that my people, which was not my people;
And her beloved, which was not beloved.
And it shall be, that in the place where it was said
unto them, Ye are not my people,
There shall they be called sons of the living God.

And Isaiah crieth concerning Israel, If the number of the children of Israel be as the sand of the sea, it is the remnant that shall be saved: for the Lord will execute his word upon the earth, finishing it and cutting it short. And, as Isaiah hath said before,

Except the Lord of Sabaoth had left us a seed,
We had become as Sodom, and had been made like
unto Gomorrah.

What has been already said will have been enough to guard against the main sources of mistake in reading this section. St. Paul might have much to say about God's righteousness in general, and large ways of vindicating it. But here he holds fast to the single aspect of righteousness according to which it means that God has been true to the original principles of His covenant. The God who chose Abraham and Moses is the God who is now, and rightly on His own declared principles of government, rejecting the greater part of the people of Abraham and Moses. This—faithfulness to His own declared principles—is what St. Paul here means by His righteousness. And as it was God's declared principle to retain His own liberty to show mercy on men according to His free will, inside or outside the chosen people, so on the other hand He retained His liberty to exhibit His judgement of hardening according to His will inside or outside the chosen people. He who brought Pharaoh the Egyptian upon the stage of history[6], as an example of hardening judgement, is within His right in doing the same now with (the mass of) the people of His choice. The liberty asserted for God is wholly consistent with His being found, in fact, to have 'hardened' those only who have deserved hardening by their own wilfulness. It was for such a moral cause that God hardened the hearts of the Jews, that 'seeing they might not see, and hearing they might not hear[7].' We can feel no doubt that some similar moral cause underlay the hardening of Pharaoh. But this is not St. Paul's present point. All his argument is directed to asserting God's liberty to show mercy or harden, irrespectively of considerations of race, when and where He in His sovereign moral will chooses.

We should notice that St. Paul's method is here, as elsewhere, what is called ideal or abstract, in the sense that he makes abstraction of a particular point of view; and, apparently indifferent to being misunderstood, substantiates his argument upon the particular aspect which he has taken apart from the whole matter in hand, till it is done with, and then other points can be taken in their turn. And he does not, as a modern writer would do, painfully correlate the various aspects of the subject[8].

By means of the famous simile of the potter St. Paul asserts two principles about God: (1) that God is free, and condescends to give no account to His creatures, in absolutely determining the high or low vocations of men. To one man or nation He gives five talents, to another two, to another one. He makes vessels to honourable and vessels to (comparatively) dishonourable uses. He makes men Jews or Assyrians, Englishmen or Hottentots, at His absolute discretion. (2) That God is absolutely free, when the human material which He is moulding for His purposes proves intractable, to repudiate and reject what has, by its refusal to mould, become a 'vessel of wrath' fit 'to be taken and destroyed.' And it is only by a voluntary limitation of this freedom that He exhibits long toleration with the intractable and obstinate, and is longsuffering with them even when His wrath is ready and waiting to show itself. These are the two distinct points in the simile of the potter. We must distinguish carefully between the 'vessels destined for dishonour'—the 'less honourable limbs' of humanity— and the 'vessels of wrath,' or 'vessels fitted for destruction,' i.e. those which have proved themselves unfit for the vocation to which they were destined and have to be rejected. We note that St. Paul does not say that God fitted vessels for destruction, but that He bore long with those which had so become fitted. St. Paul never gives us any real justification—if we look at his language carefully—for the idea of any predestination to rejection, as distinct from predestination to higher or lower purposes. And the New Testament is full of assurances that a predestination to a low vocation in this world may be a predestination to high glory in eternity, if the humble calling is faithfully followed.

It ought not to be denied, however, that in all this passage St. Paul's feet, as he moves along his argument, are dogged by the metaphysical difficulty of finding room for human free-will inside the universal scope of the divine action and the prescience of the divine wisdom. This is a perennial difficulty. But St. Paul does not touch it. He does not even touch the question of whether God does actually (in our sense) foreknow the final destiny of every individual, and how he will act on each occasion[9]; he does not touch the question how or how far human wilfulness can be allowed to disturb the divine order. In the Pharisaic schools he would certainly have been brought up, as Josephus tells us, both to 'attribute everything to fate and God,' and also to recognize that it 'lay with men for the most part to do right or wrong': to believe that 'everything was foreseen,' and also that 'free-will was given'; or, as Josephus elsewhere puts it (as if it made no difference), to believe 'that some things, but not all, are the work of fate, and other things are in men's own power and need not happen[10].' That is to say, he would have been educated to believe both in predestination and in freedom, without any special attempt to reconcile the two. We can tell for certain that this inherited belief was further moralized in St. Paul's case by his enlarged view of the divine purpose as working through high and low estates alike, for the final good of all men; and by his deepened perception of the correspondence with God's purpose, which, in the exercise of our freedom, is required of us. But, so far as we know, St. Paul left the strictly metaphysical question exactly where he found it—as an imperfectly reconciled antithesis. And there perhaps we men shall always have to leave it, or at least till we come to know even as we are known.

In the quotations from the Old Testament, with which the section concludes, we notice that St. Paul varies the original application of the passages from Hosea. In the prophet they refer to the recovery of dejected and dishonoured Israel, while the apostle applies them to the exaltation of the Gentiles from their low estate. As is often the case, while other passages in the prophets were there to prove exactly what he wanted[11], St. Paul takes the words which come into his mind with a considerable latitude of application, and without any critical argument. Thus, if he makes somewhat free with the particular texts, it is in order to vindicate the real teaching of the Old Testament. He has, if not exact criticism, what is much better, profound spiritual insight.

The passages quoted from Isaiah are characteristic and central. This great prophet first clearly perceived that most striking law of human history—

that progress comes, not mostly through the majority of a nation, but through the faithful remnant. It is the few best through whom alone God can freely work. It is the best who in the long run determine the moral level of the nation, and either keep the mass of men around them from corruption, or, if that is impossible, provide a fresh point of departure and hope in a society now inevitably, as a whole, hastening to decay and judgement. 'As a terebinth, and as an oak, whose stock remaineth, when they are felled; so the holy seed is the stock thereof[12].'

[1] Isa. xxix. 16, xlv. 9, lxiv. 8; Jer. xviii. 6; Ecclus. xxxiii. 13.

[2] xv. 7.

[3] 1 Cor. xii. 22-5; 2 Tim. ii. 20.

[4] Jer. xviii. 4. The passage continues with a strong assertion of God's freedom to govern the destinies of nations on moral principles.

[5] When Moses asked to see God's glory (Exod. xxxiii. 18), what was revealed to him was His goodness and free mercy, and what St. Paul here means by God's glory is His mercy especially.

[6] In the original the words run, 'For this cause have I made thee to stand,' i.e. probably, 'I have preserved thy life under the plague of boils, and other plagues, in order to make thee an example of a more conspicuous judgement.' But St. Paul, departing from the Greek Bible, uses a word 'raised thee up,' which in Pharaoh's case, or in that of Cyrus, means to bring upon the stage of history. Isa. xli. 2; cf. Jer. 1. [xxvii in the Greek] 41; Hab. i. 6.

[7] See Matt. xiii. 14, 15; Mark iv. 12; John xii. 40.

[8] Cf. vol. i. p. 75.

[9] On the meaning of divine foreknowledge in St. Paul see vol. i. p. 317.

[10] See Joseph. Antiq. xiii. 5, 9; xviii. 1, 3; Bell. Jud. ii. 8, 14. Cf. Schürer, Jewish People (English trans.), Div. ii. vol. ii. pp.14 ff.; James and Ryle, Ps. of Solomon, p. 96. The Essenes, Josephus says, believed in fate, and not in free-will; the Sadducees in free-will and not in fate; but the Pharisees in both. No doubt Josephus is importing Greek philosophical views into his account of Jewish parties, but substantially his account is probably true.

[11] e.g. Isa. xix. 24; Ezek. xvi. 55. (The exaltation into the fellowship of the chosen people of Egypt, Assyria, Sodom, and Samaria.)

[12] Isa. vi. 13.

DIVISION IV. § 3. CHAPTER IX. 30-X. 21.

Lack of faith the reason of Israel's rejection.

What is to be our conclusion then? That Gentiles, men beyond the pale of God's covenant, who made no pretension of pursuing righteousness, all at once laid hold on righteousness and made it their own, simply by accepting in faith the divine offer which came their way; while Israel, the chosen people, devoted to pursuing a law of righteousness, never caught up with that of which it was in pursuit. The result seems strange enough. But the reason of it is apparent. Israel[1] had been put under a divine election, which required of them the open ear, the responsive will, of faith. But instead of cultivating this temper of faith, they fastened upon the specified observances of the Mosaic law, and blindly adhered to them, as if God had nothing deeper or greater to teach them, and they had nothing deeper or greater to receive. Thus, when the Christ came, with His completer light and claims, they would not have Him. They wanted nothing further, nothing more than they were accustomed to. And thus Isaiah's prophecy was fulfilled, that the Christ, the tried foundation stone, the destined security of all who should believe in Him, would turn out to be a stone at which the chosen people should stumble, and a rock on which it should meet disaster[2] (ix. 30-33).

And here is the pathos of the situation. Here is what puts passion into St. Paul's desire and his prayer for Israel's entrance into the great deliverance. It is that they have such a real zeal for God, though without any spiritual insight to guide it. A real zeal for God! of that St. Paul's own experience qualified him to testify. But in what sense without insight? In the sense that with Jesus of Nazareth there appeared a divine righteousness, which God was communicating to men[3]; but the Jews, preoccupied with maintaining a standard of righteousness which they had taken for their own—which had become identified, that is to say, with their own self-satisfaction and pride of privilege and independence of interference—failed to perceive the divine purpose, and, in fact, refused to submit themselves to it. For that principle of law which the Jews had come to regard as God's final word, He really intended only as a temporary discipline to be brought to an end by the coming of the Christ, and by the disclosure of the real righteousness which, in Christ, God should offer and man should simply accept in faith. Law and faith are in sharp and intelligible contrast. Under the law of works a man, as Moses says[4], stands to preserve his life (or save his soul) according as he performs the specified requirements (as if man were an independent being who could thus stand over against God on his merits).

But faith, attributing nothing to itself, simply accepts the offer of God, the divine message of compassion brought near to it. Moses of old told the Israelites[5] that the commandment was not too hard for them, neither was it far off. It was not in heaven, that they should say, who shall go up for us to heaven, and bring it unto us, and make us to hear it, that we may do it? Neither was it beyond the sea, that they should say, who shall go over the sea for us, and bring it unto us, and make us to hear it that we may do it? But the word was very nigh unto them, in their mouth and in their heart, that they might do it. These words really describe the character of the Christian message of faith, of which the apostles are the heralds. Truly there is no need for the believer in Jesus to seek some one to scale heaven to reach a remote God, for Christ is come down. Or to descend into the abyss to seek a Christ dead and lost, for Christ is risen. The great deliverance is offered to us on very easy terms. A man has only openly to confess that the human Jesus is really the divine Lord, and heartily to believe that God raised Him from the dead. Let him heartily accept that message, and the fellowship in the divine righteousness is his. Let him publicly confess that creed, and the great salvation is open to him. It is the old teaching of Isaiah[6]—if a man but believe (in the Christ) there is no fear of his being put to shame. And here Jews and Greeks are all on the same level of need and opportunity. There is over all the same Lord Christ, with the same inexhaustible good will towards all who simply call on Him. Again the old scripture testifies that it is every one who calls on the name of the Lord who shall be saved[7]. The conditions then are very simple. To call on the Lord, we may say, men must believe in Him. To have the opportunity of believing on Him, they must have heard about Him. To hear about Him, they need one to speak in His name. And how can men speak in the name of God except as His apostles, as men commissioned and sent from Him? And these terms we know well enough have all been fulfilled. The commissioned heralds of the good tidings of God have gone forth, so that all men may hear and believe and call out to God. Truly Isaiah's vision of the welcome preacher of good tidings[8] is realized to-day (x. 1-15).

Now we have clear before us the simplicity of the gospel, the message to faith. And we have before us the plain fact that the Israelitish people, preoccupied with their own temporary and misunderstood standard of the law, have not generally accepted it. But this is no more than Isaiah led us to expect. 'Lord,' he cries, 'who gave credence to our message[9]?' (Faith, you see, according to the prophet, requires just a listening to a divine message; and this message has come to men by the preaching about Christ.) And can it be pleaded that the Jews have not had the opportunity of hearing the message? No, truly, as the Psalmist says, the voice of God's messengers has gone over all the earth, and their words to the end of the inhabited world[10]. Or can it be said that Israel did not know that a preaching to the Gentiles was to be looked for? No, a succession of warnings had reached them. Thus Moses foretold that it should be a nation which (religiously speaking) was no nation, a people without understanding, that God would use to provoke His people to jealousy, and stimulate their emulation[11]. Again, Isaiah uses startling words, and declares that God has been discovered by those who never sought Him, and revealed to those who never asked for Him[12]—that is the Gentiles. But the words of Isaiah that follow describe truly the relation of God and Israel. God has tenderly and persistently been offering His love to them, but they have proved themselves only rebellious and full of contradiction (x. 16-21).

This, then, is the plain summary. Israel is rejected because, after every offer, and with every opportunity, they have refused God's leading, refused to be docile, refused to believe, refused to obey.

What shall we say then? That the Gentiles, which followed not after righteousness, attained to righteousness, even the righteousness which is of faith: but Israel, following after a law of righteousness, did not arrive at that law. Wherefore? Because they sought it not by faith, but as it were by works. They stumbled at the stone of stumbling; even as it is written,

Behold, I lay in Zion a stone of stumbling and a rock of offence: And he that believeth on him shall not be put to shame.

Brethren, my heart's desire and my supplication to God is for them, that they may be saved. For I bear them witness that they have a zeal for God, but not according to knowledge. For being ignorant of God's righteousness, and seeking to establish their own, they did not subject themselves to the righteousness of God. For Christ is the end of the law unto righteousness to every one that believeth. For Moses writeth that the man that doeth the righteousness which is of the law shall live thereby. But the righteousness which is of faith saith thus, Say not in thy heart, Who shall ascend into heaven? (that is, to bring Christ down:) or, Who shall descend into the abyss? (that is, to bring Christ up from the dead.) But what saith it? The word is nigh thee, in thy mouth, and in thy heart: that is, the word of faith, which we preach: because if thou shalt confess with thy mouth Jesus as Lord, and shalt believe in thy heart that God raised him from the dead, thou shalt be saved: for with the heart man believeth unto righteousness; and with the mouth confession is made unto salvation. For the scripture saith, Whosoever believeth on him shall not be put to shame. For there is no distinction between Jew and Greek: for the same Lord is Lord of all, and is rich unto all that call upon him: for, Whosoever shall call upon the name of the Lord shall be saved. How then shall they call on him in whom they have not believed? and how shall they believe in him whom they have not heard? and how shall they hear without a preacher? and how shall they preach, except they be sent? even as it is written, How beautiful are the feet of them that bring glad tidings of good things!

But they did not all hearken to the glad tidings. For Isaiah saith, Lord, who hath believed our report? So belief cometh of hearing, and hearing by the word of Christ. But I say, Did they not hear? Yea, verily,

Their sound went out into all the earth,
And their words unto the ends of the world.

But I say, Did Israel not know? First Moses saith,

I will provoke you to jealousy with that which is no nation,
With a nation void of understanding will I anger you.

And Isaiah is very bold, and saith,

I was found of them that sought me not;
I became manifest unto them that asked not of me.

But as to Israel he saith, All the day long did I spread out my hands unto a disobedient and gainsaying people.

In this passage St. Paul gives us the other side of the question of the rejection of the Israelites. God had retained an absolute freedom, not to be questioned by men, to reject whom He willed. That was the first point. But can we see whom our God wills to reject, or why in particular He rejected (though not finally, as will appear) the chosen people? It is because they failed in faith. And faith is precisely that which is necessary to maintain correspondence with God—it is the faculty of fellowship with Him. They failed because the false principle of justification by works had obscured in their minds the need and meaning of faith. The false principle meant, as we have already seen, the maintaining an accepted standard of conduct and divine service, especially in outward matters, and for the rest claiming to be left alone. The accepted standard was that which distinguished Israel from the rest of the world, and what they had become accustomed to. It was a righteousness of 'their own.' They prided themselves on it. Their public opinion required its observance. It had come to usurp the place of any direct relationship to the voice of God. They had no idea that God could have anything more or deeper to require of them. They had lost personal touch with Him. Therefore seeking to establish this, their own righteousness, they failed to submit themselves to the (now newly revealed) righteousness of God in Christ. This unprogressiveness of the Jewish ideal, this substitution of the accepted standard under the law for the word of God, on the part of the Pharisees, the religious representatives of Israel, is precisely what the pages of the Gospel record. Therefore the 'corner stone of sure foundation' for the divine building became to them the stone on which they stumbled and fell. And yet that the law was a temporary expedient, and not the whole counsel of God, was the deepest witness of the Old Testament; and in being false to the further revelation of the will of God in Christ, they were false to their own deepest principles. All this ground we have gone over already, and need not traverse again[13].

So also we have already become familiar with the simplicity of the message of God in Christ, and the simplicity of the faith which, rooted in the consciousness of sin and need, and equally possible for all men who can share this consciousness, is required to welcome God's offer, and so be brought by Christ into living union with Him. All this St. Paul has already elaborated, and is here only resuming and recapitulating by the way. But one or two points in the recapitulation require notice.

1. St. Paul takes the basis of his statement of the principle of grace and faith out of the heart of the books of Moses—the idea of the 'word very nigh thee,' of the simple message claiming only to be simply accepted, and of the 'very present help' of a gracious God needing only to be welcomed. The fact is that St. Paul usually idealizes when he treats of 'the law of Moses'; as, for example, when he here says that 'Moses writeth that the man that doeth the righteousness ... shall live thereby,' as if that was all that Moses said. The principle of law, as Saul the Pharisee had learned to understand it, is the dominant principle in the five Books of the Law, but not the only one. 'Grace, already existing in the Jewish theocracy, was the fruitful germ deposited under the surface, which was one day to burst forth and become the peculiar character of the new covenant[14].' The God of the new covenant is the God also of the old, and was there already intimating His truer and deeper character. To this St. Paul bears witness by resting his statement of the principle of the new covenant upon the words of the old.

2. In this passage we have the germ of what we call the creed. The lordship of Jesus, in the sense which implies His proper divinity, and His resurrection and triumph over death—was already matter of public confession in the Christian church: to make profession that 'Jesus is Lord' qualified for 'the salvation'[15]: and in this lay hid all that is essential to the Christian creed. Already then in the earliest church subjective faith involved a certain objective and public creed[16] which came very soon to be called 'the faith.' In this passage also, as in xiv. 9 and in St. Peter's epistle, we recognize, as an element in the common tradition, the belief in the Descent into Hades (the abyss).

3. St. Paul incidentally shows us his instinctive feeling that to be a trustworthy ambassador for God one needs 'apostolate.' 'How shall they preach except they be sent?' And this apostolate, as he uses it, means not

only an inward sense of mission, but an external sending by Christ Himself; and in pursuance of the same principle, when once the Church has been established, it would mean a sending by those authorized to send in His name. This is the root principle of the Christian 'stewardship.' As the subapostolic Clement expresses it, 'Christ (was sent) from God, and the apostles from Christ. Each came in due order from the will of God. Therefore, having received the words of command, and having been fully convinced by the resurrection of our Lord Jesus Christ, and been assured in the message of God with conviction of the Holy Ghost, they came forth, preaching the gospel that the kingdom of God was to come. Therefore as they preached in country and towns they established their first-fruits, when they had put them to the proof, to be bishops (i.e. presbyters), and deacons of those who were to come to the faith.' And afterwards, in view of disputes over the presbyteral office, which divine inspiration enabled them to anticipate, they made provision for a due succession in the 'episcopate' on the death of those first appointed[17].

4. St. Paul's singularly free, but deeply inspired, manner of applying texts from the Old Testament is especially illustrated in this passage.

Thus the passages quoted from Isaiah about the Stone, which St. Paul applies to Christ, refer originally to Jehovah simply in one case (Isa. viii. 14), and probably to His will and covenant as the foundation of Israel's polity in the other (Isa. xxviii. 16). Jewish tradition had possibly already referred them to the Christ[18]; and certainly our Lord's use of Ps. cxviii. 22—'The stone which the builders rejected'—as applying to His own rejection, made the reference more obvious. It is indeed in deepest accordance with the spirit of Isaiah: and St. Peter (1 Peter ii. 6), we notice, follows St. Paul in the use of them. Another passage (lii. 7) about 'the feet of those who preach good tidings' is transferred, with added meaning, from the heralds of the redemption from Babylon, to the heralds of the greater redemption. And the opening of chapter lxv, which originally refers altogether to apostate Israel, is divided, and applied in part to the Gentiles, in part to the Jews. (Other passages in the prophets, we should observe, would justify the former application.) Again, a passage from Ps. xix is transferred very beautifully from the witness of the heavens to the witness of the Gospel; as if St. Paul would say—grace is become as universal as nature. The language of a passage from Deuteronomy, as we have seen, is taken from the law to express the spirit of the gospel. The calling upon Jehovah in Joel becomes in St. Paul's quotation the calling upon Christ. All this free citation, uncritical according to our ideas and methods, yet rests upon a profoundly right apprehension of the meaning of the Old Testament as a whole. The appeal to the Old Testament, even if not to the particular passage, is justified by the strictest criticism.

[1] I have endeavoured sometimes in this analysis to expand what St. Paul means by 'pursuing righteousness,' by 'works' and by 'faith,' in accordance with the meaning already assigned to these words; see vol. i. pp. 7-24.

[2] Isa. viii. 14; xxviii. 16. Cf. Matt. xi. 6.

[3] See above, vol. i. p. 17.

[4] Levit. xviii. 5.

[5] Deut. xxx. 11-14. I have italicized the words substantially reproduced by St. Paul, but I have quoted the whole passage because its whole meaning is in his mind.

[6] Isa. xxviii. 16.

[7] Joel ii. 32.

[8] Isa. lii. 7.

[9] Isa. liii. 1.

[10] Ps. xix. 4.

[11] Deut. xxxii. 21.

[12] Isa. lxv. 1, 2.

[13] See vol. i. pp. 7 ff., 165 f., 250 ff.

[14] Godet in loc.

[15] Cf. 1 Cor. xii. 3. The lordship of Jesus, we see in this passage, means that He can have applied to Him the sayings of the Old Testament about the Lord Jehovah; and can be 'called upon' as such in prayer (Joel ii. 32).

[16] Cf. 1 Cor. xv. 1-3.

[17] Clem, ad Cor. 42, 44.

[18] See S. and H. in loc.

DIVISION IV. § 4. CHAPTER XI. 1-12.

God's judgement on Israel neither universal nor final.

But if Israel has thus by her own fault fallen from her high estate, are we then to suppose that God has simply rejected His own chosen people? Such a thought cannot be entertained. How could it have been in the mind of such an Israelite as St. Paul, one who came of Abraham's genuine seed, and of the tribe which held so fast by Judah? No: the people on whom from eternity God's eye rested, to mark them out for Himself and for His purposes, assuredly cannot, as a people, have been cast away[1]. What has happened now is only what is recorded long ago in the history of Elijah. Then, as now, a general unfaithfulness in the bulk of the nation concealed the existence of a faithful remnant. Yet God had, as He assured the prophet, reserved for Himself such a remnant, and of very considerable numbers. And now also such a remnant of true Israelites exists in accordance with the selective action of grace—that is to say, God's gratuitous and unmerited good will. Yes: let there be no mistake about it; their position is due to nothing else than the original and continuous action of God's grace; and grace means God's absolutely gratuitous and unmerited good will (which may therefore come upon Gentiles equally with Jews). It excludes the idea of these remnants owing their position to previous merits, or of its being in any way God's response to an antecedent claim[2].

This then is what we have to recognize. What Israel in bulk sought for (by way of its supposed merit), that it did not get, but a select remnant got it; and upon the rest there fell that judicial hardening—that reversal of their true relation to God—which Moses and Isaiah already discerned in the chosen people[3]: an abiding stupor, and deafness, and blindness, with regard to God's purpose and will for them. David too, as God's righteous servant, demands, as a divine requital upon his bitter and cruel enemies, that their very abundance should betray them into captivity and prove their stumblingblock; that their spiritual vision should be lost and their backs bent downward to the ground. Which is just what has happened to Israel through their rejection of the Son of David.

The bulk of the people then has stumbled. But we must not exaggerate what has happened. As it is not all of them who have stumbled, so also it is not for ever. Their stumbling is not equivalent to a final fall. Already we can perceive how it may be reversed. The refusal of the Jews to recognize the Christ has been the occasion for a turning to the Gentiles. Thus the salvation of the Christ has come to them. And this has happened in the divine providence in order that, as Moses anticipated, they may in their turn provoke the Jews to jealousy—to a jealous determination not to lose their old privileges. Thus if even the transgression of Israel has proved the occasion for enriching the world as a whole, if even the deficiency of Israel (leaving vacant space, as it were, in the Church) has proved the occasion for enriching the Gentiles, how much more enrichment is to be expected when the chosen people are recovered in their full number?

I say then, Did God cast off his people? God forbid. For I also am an Israelite, of the seed of Abraham, of the tribe of Benjamin. God did not cast off his people which he foreknew. Or wot ye not what the scripture saith of Elijah[4]? how he pleadeth with God against Israel, Lord, they have killed thy prophets, they have digged down thine altars: and I am left alone, and they seek my life. But what saith the answer of God unto him? I have left for myself seven thousand men, who have not bowed the knee to Baal. Even so then at this present time also there is a remnant according to the election of grace. But if it is by grace, it is no more of works: otherwise grace is no more grace. What then? That which Israel seeketh for, that he obtained not; but the election obtained it, and the rest were hardened: according as it is written, God gave them a spirit of stupor, eyes that they should not see, and ears that they should not hear, unto this very day. And David saith,

Let their table be made a snare, and a trap,
And a stumblingblock, and a recompense unto them:
Let their eyes be darkened, that they may not see,
And bow thou down their back alway.

I say then, Did they stumble that they might fall? God forbid: but by their fall salvation is come unto the Gentiles, for to provoke them to jealousy. Now if their fall is the riches of the world, and their loss the riches of the Gentiles; how much more their fulness?

1. We learn a little more exactly about St. Paul's doctrine of election in this chapter. God's final purpose for good is, as we shall see at the end of the chapter—and in what sense we shall have to consider—upon all men whatsoever. But this universal purpose is worked out through special 'elect' instruments. Thus God recognized[5] Israel beforehand, i.e. in His eternal counsels, as the people to bear His name in the world. This was the selection of Israel, and was an act of which the initiative was wholly on God's side. It was a pure act of the divine favour. This 'selection of grace' was upon Israel as a whole, but at later stages of the history, frequently enough, owing to the disobedience and apostasy of the majority, it is found to rest in an effective sense only upon a 'remnant' whom God has reserved for Himself, because they have not utterly refused to correspond to the original and continuous call of the divine grace. For the rest their privileges

become the occasion of their fall: their light becomes their darkness. For judgement always and inevitably waits upon any form of misused privilege. Thus, when the Christ came, only an elect remnant of the nation welcomed Him. The rest fell under judgement. But God overrules even this apostasy. He takes the opportunity of the absence of those who should have been at the marriage supper of the king's son, to fill the great vacancy from the Gentile world. They are brought within the scope of the selecting call. But God's original vocation is still irrevocably upon apostate Israel. The new Gentile converts are to stimulate them to recover their lost privileges. Their wilfulness and obstinacy is to give place to humility and faith; and Jew and Gentile all together are to constitute the elect catholic church.

This is very simple and cheerful teaching. It leaves for us to consider later the question whether God's original and special vocation resting upon the Jews is finally to constrain them all to conversion, and whether in the same way His ultimate purpose of salvation for all men is to take place infallibly in all cases. This question is still to be considered. But at any rate the doctrine of election has lost all that gave it a colouring of arbitrariness and injustice and narrow sympathies.

We ought to notice in the above passage how St. Paul, in recalling the continual obstinacy and hardening of the majority of the chosen people, is following on the lines of St. Stephen's speech (Acts vii. 51).

2. The imprecatory psalms are, especially in our Anglican public services, a great stumblingblock to many—especially the 69th (here cited by St. Paul) and the 109th. These psalms do not represent barely the cry of an individual sufferer invoking God's curse upon his private enemies. The sufferer, who is the psalmist, or with whom at least the psalmist identifies himself, represents afflicted righteousness. It is God's people, His 'servant' and 'son' according to the language of the Old Testament, that is under persecution from the enemies of God. And he calls upon God to vindicate Himself by punishing the adversary; to let it be seen that His word and promise is truth. 'How long, O God, holy and true, dost thou not judge and avenge?' Even from this point of view, however, when with the assistance of the modern critics we have in the main purged away the element of private vindictiveness, these psalms no doubt remain with the stamp of narrowness and bitterness upon them. They have none of the larger New Testament sense that the worst enemies of the Church may be converted and live: that our attitude towards all men is to wish them good, purely good and not evil, even though it be under the form of judgement: 'Rejoice when men revile you and persecute you'; 'Bless them that curse you, do good to them that hate you, pray for them which despitefully use you'; 'That by your good works which they shall behold, they may glorify God in the day of visitation.'

But granted the limitation and bitterness still remaining in these psalms, their citation in the New Testament shows us what is for us the right use of them. They are by implication taken up—where we should least expect them—into the mouth of the Son of Man[6]. That is to say, it is His enemies on whom the judgements are imprecated. There is a wrath of the Lamb. There is a divine sword of judgement which proceeds out of His mouth. He, the administrator of the righteousness of God, expects from His Father judgement on His enemies. It is not necessarily, as St. Paul here indicates, final judgement: the judgement upon the Jews was not yet that; but judgement of some sort—temporal or final—upon His wilful adversaries, the Son expects of the Father. And we men, as we repeat these psalms, are, like the first Christians in face of the suicide of Judas, to identify ourselves with the divine righteousness and accept the law of just retribution. This is the deepest and truest sense in which we can still say the imprecatory psalms; and in these days of a philanthropy that often lacks the stern savour of righteousness, it is very necessary that we should make this sense our own.

[1] Three times—1 Sam. xii. 22, Ps. xciv. 14, xcv. 3 (in the Greek)—the promise occurs 'The Lord will not cast away His people.'

[2] The vocation and election which made Israel the chosen people were absolutely of God. What distinguished the faithful remnant from the bulk of the nation was simply that they had not altogether failed in faith, so that the unchanging election was not in their cases practically suspended, but God 'reserved them for Himself.'

[3] St. Paul refers chiefly to Isa. xxix. 10—the description of a besotted people whose prophets are eyes that cannot see, and their seers ears that cannot hear; so that the word of God has become as a sealed book; cf. also Isa. vi. 9. But there is a similar passage in Deut. xxix. 4, which partly moulds his language, and supplies the words 'unto this day.'

[4] Rather, as margin, in Elijah, i.e. the passage of Scripture about Elijah.

[5] This—to recognize or mark out beforehand—is the meaning of divine 'foreknowing' in St. Paul. See vol. i. pp. 317 f.

[6] Both in this passage and in Acts i. 20.

DIVISION IV. § 5[1]. CHAPTER XI. 13-36.

God's present purpose for the Jews through the Gentiles: and so for all humanity.

St. Paul would not have it supposed that, in his zeal for the recovery of Israel, he was proving faithless to his vocation as the apostle of the Gentiles. On the contrary, he explains (assuming the Roman Christians to be Gentiles in the mass) that he is, by this very zeal, fulfilling that vocation. The conversion of the Gentiles was meant to react as a stimulus on the Jews. When St. Paul magnifies his Gentile ministry, he does so always with the motive of stinging the jealousy of his own people, and so bringing some of them to salvation. How can such a consummation be too eagerly desired? For if even so pitiable an event as their rejection has yet, in God's providence, been overruled for a good end—the bringing back of the outside world into the fellowship of God[2]: can we doubt that so happy an event as their recovery would be indeed (what Ezekiel saw in vision in the valley of the dry bones) a veritable resurrection? For the consecration of God is still upon them. The holy (i.e. consecrated) people they still remain. As the 'heave offering' of the 'first of the dough'[3] consecrates the whole lump, so the first of the nation offered to God—Abraham, Isaac, and Jacob—have consecrated the whole nation. The holiness of the root of God's olive tree[4] has passed to the latest branches. It is quite true that some of these branches of the Jewish olive tree were broken off, and that the Gentiles were introduced in their place; like a wild olive grafted upon the root of a cultivated plant, and so sharing its rich sap. But that—to let the metaphor continue—gives the wild olive no ground for an insolent contempt of the branches which naturally belonged to the tree. What advantage it now has it wholly derives from that which it is affecting to despise. It is the root that supports it, not it the root. And are the Gentiles disposed to argue that these rejected Jewish branches were broken off in order that they might take their place; and that they, the Gentiles, are thus plainly preferred by God to the Jews? The answer is plain. Why were they broken off? Because they would not maintain the correspondence of faith with the purpose of God; and it is simply by maintaining this attitude that the newly introduced Gentiles can hope to retain their place. They had better exhibit, not a groundless pride, but a reasonable fear. Is God likely to be more sparing towards them than towards His first chosen? God has displayed before their eyes both His attributes of severity and goodness, and they must take note of both. At the present moment it is severity towards Jews, goodness towards Gentiles. Yes, goodness towards Gentiles;

but so long only as they abide faithfully in His goodness, no longer. When they fail of faithfulness, they too, like their Jewish predecessors, shall be cut off. And, on the other hand, when those Jews change their attitude, and their hardness melts and faith returns, they shall be recovered and reingrafted into the old olive tree. If God could graft into it branches cut out of an alien and inferior stock, how much more easily can He reingraft into it what is really part of its very self?

Here then we have a real disclosure of a divine secret[5], to which the Gentiles would do well to keep their eyes open, lest (like the Jews before them) they mistake for wisdom their own self-conceit. The hardening of the Jews has been used by God as an opportunity for the gathering in of the full number of the nations of the earth; and that with the further purpose that, when the nations are gathered in, Israel in all its completeness should be recovered too. And so shall be fulfilled Isaiah's prophecy of a redeemer from Zion, who should restore Israel, and of a new covenant with them, based on a fresh forgiveness of their sins[6]. Thus if we think of the actual relation of the Jews to the present preaching of the Gospel, we must think of them as God's enemies, and as having by their very enmity secured the Gentiles their opportunity; but if we think of them in relation to God's eternal choice, they still must appear as sharing the divine love which rests on the people of Abraham, Isaac, and Jacob. God's gifts and vocation do not admit of being repented of and recalled. Thus we know what to expect. As the Gentiles passed out from disobedience under the divine compassion through the opportunity afforded by the disobedience of the Jews; so now the divine compassion which rests on the Gentiles is intended (by stimulating the Jews to recover their lost privileges) to prove the means of recovering them too out of their disobedience into the shelter of the divine compassion which is the common heritage of all. We see, in fact, all men in turn shut up in disobedience to God, as in a prison house: it is God who has so shut them up; but it is done in view of the largest and most compassionate purpose which can be even conceived. It is done that (when men have become wearied of their own wilfulness, and have experienced their own need) the divine mercy may welcome and embrace all alike at last.

And if this is the purpose of God disclosed to us, how can we fail to adore the fathomless resourcefulness of His wisdom in determining how to act, and His skill in executing what He has determined? How can we fail to recognize our utter incompetence to explore His judgement, or track out His ways? Like inspired men of old[7] we must recognize that the absolute initiative is His, and our only reasonable attitude the humblest correspondence. Truly in counsel and operation we have contributed to God nothing of our own: we have no claim with which to approach Him.

He is the unique source of whatever is, and the sole executor of whatever takes place, and the only end to which all things tend: and to Him, therefore, alone all praise is due, and shall be given.

But I speak to you that are Gentiles. Inasmuch then as I am an apostle of Gentiles, I glorify my ministry: if by any means I may provoke to jealousy them that are my flesh, and may save some of them. For if the casting away of them is the reconciling of the world, what shall the receiving of them be, but life from the dead? And if the firstfruit is holy, so is the lump: and if the root is holy, so are the branches. But if some of the branches were broken off, and thou, being a wild olive, wast grafted in among them, and didst become partaker with them of the root of the fatness of the olive tree; glory not over the branches: but if thou gloriest, it is not thou that bearest the root, but the root thee. Thou wilt say then, Branches were broken off, that I might be grafted in. Well; by their unbelief they were broken off, and thou standest by thy faith. Be not highminded, but fear: for if God spared not the natural branches, neither will he spare thee. Behold then the goodness and severity of God: toward them that fell, severity; but toward thee, God's goodness, if thou continue in his goodness: otherwise thou also shalt be cut off. And they also, if they continue not in their unbelief, shall be grafted in: for God is able to graft them in again. For if thou wast cut out of that which is by nature a wild olive tree, and wast grafted contrary to nature into a good olive tree: how much more shall these, which are the natural branches, be grafted into their own olive tree?

For I would not, brethren, have you ignorant of this mystery, lest ye be wise in your own conceits, that a hardening in part hath befallen Israel, until the fulness of the Gentiles be come in; and so all Israel shall be saved, even as it is written,

There shall come out of Zion the Deliverer;
He shall turn away ungodliness from Jacob:
And this is my covenant unto them,
When I shall take away their sins.

As touching the gospel, they are enemies for your sake: but as touching the election, they are beloved for the fathers' sake. For the gifts and the calling of God are without repentance. For as ye in time past were disobedient to God, but now have obtained mercy by their disobedience, even so have these also now been disobedient, that by the mercy shewn to you they also may now obtain mercy. For God hath shut up all unto disobedience, that he might have mercy upon all.

O the depth of the riches both of the wisdom and the knowledge of God! how unsearchable are his judgements, and his ways past tracing out! For who hath known the mind of the Lord? or who hath been his counsellor?

or who hath first given to him, and it shall be recompensed unto him again? For of him, and through him, and unto him, are all things. To him be the glory for ever. Amen.

1. There is a true patriotism which must at times be content to wear the guise of disloyalty; and not even Jeremiah 'weakening the hands of the men of war[8]' in the conflict with the power of Babylon, while all the time his very heart was bleeding for Jerusalem, presents a more pathetic and moving picture of such patriotism than does St. Paul as he here shows himself to us. While he was shaking off the dust of his feet, as he left the synagogues to turn to the Gentiles, while he was throwing all his tremendous energy into the apostolate of the nations, and vindicating their cause, even to fierceness, against the narrowness of his own nation, all the time the thought which buoyed him up was that when the catholic church had become an established fact—when it should have become plain, even to Jewish eyes, that the elect people of God is now a fraternity of all nations, and not their own race only—then it could not fail to happen, that the members of the ancient people, finding themselves in their turn 'alienated,' 'strangers,' and 'far off,' while they knew so well, and needed so deeply, the fellowship of the covenant, should be stimulated to resume their former privileges. Surely then at last Israel 'should remember her way and be ashamed,' and 'receive' her Gentile 'sisters,' though they had been to her as 'Sodom and Samaria,' and though they were now given to her for 'daughters, but not by her covenant'—not by any means on her own terms[9]. All the time that St. Paul is fighting Judaism and vindicating Catholicism, laying down the lines of the great church of the nations, this is the vision that cheers him—an Israel, penitent, humbled, worshipping the Christ whom she had crucified, and therefore welcomed back again with the honour due to her great memories and her inextinguishable vocation. But we notice by the way, as throwing an unmistakable light on the circumstances of Roman Christianity, that while St. Paul thus shows his own Jewish feeling, he speaks to the Roman Christian as in the mass Gentile[10].

2. If so miserable an event, one so revolting to the divine heart, as the apostasy of Israel, had yet in the determinate counsel and foreknowledge of God been overruled so as to become the occasion for the calling of the Gentiles, it must needs be, St. Paul argues, that an event so dear to the heart of God as the recovery of Israel, would have a result even more blessed, nothing less than 'life from the dead.' What does this last expression mean? Does St. Paul mean that when once the chosen people was recovered into a really catholic church, there would be no further delay—the consummation would be reached, the resurrection of the dead which is to accompany the (second) coming of the Christ would take place

at once? This thought would be very natural to St. Paul, and thoroughly agreeable to the old Messianic expectation; and it would give, as nothing else gives so well, the needed climax to the sentence. Moreover it cannot be said that the idea of the resurrection was not intimately associated among Christians with the return of the Christ in glory. But, on the other hand, nowhere else does St. Paul speak of 'the resurrection' so absolutely and without explanation as the goal of all things; and, if he had meant so to speak of it here, he would surely have said 'the resurrection,' and not used the vaguer expression 'life from the dead.' As he has used this we must interpret it in terms of Ezekiel's vision[11]: the recovery of Israel will be nothing less than a case of dead men coming to life again, of dry bones revivified. The only drawback to this interpretation is—what need not trouble us much—the failure of rhetorical climax. This revival of dead Israel is hardly a greater thing than the reconciliation of an alienated world. And, though it would improve the rhetorical climax to interpret the phrase as meaning that the whole catholic church would have new life put into it by Israel's recovery, and though we should expect this idea to prove true, yet I do not think it is natural to introduce it here.

3. St. Paul's language—'beloved for the fathers' sake,' 'if the root be holy, so are the branches'—comes very close to the current Jewish language about 'the merits of the fathers,' and yet is deeply distinguished from it. The Jews as represented in the Talmud—and the belief goes back to St. Paul's time[12]—believed that no prayer was so effective as that which was offered in the name of 'the fathers.' Thus: 'How many prayers did Elijah speak on Mount Carmel that fire might fall from heaven, and he was not heard; but when he mentioned the name of the dead, and called Jehovah the God of Abraham, Isaac and Jacob, then at once he was heard. So was it in the case of Moses. When the Israelites had accomplished that bad work, Moses stood up and spoke for their justification forty days and forty nights, and was not heard. But when he mentioned the dead, he was at once heard.... Therefore as the living vine supports itself on a dead stock (i.e. grows out of a stock dry and seemingly dead), so Israel lives and supports itself on the fathers since they are dead[13].' The individual Israelite, moreover, could supply his own deficiencies in righteousness out of the treasury of merits which belonged to him in virtue of his descent from the common fathers of the race, or the holy progenitors of his own family. In other words the Israelites in various ways and senses depended for salvation on having 'Abraham to their father.' And it has already appeared sufficiently how dangerous this belief was; and how utterly St. Paul, like Ezekiel[14] and John the Baptist before him, repudiated this idea of genealogical and traditional merit as a ground of confidence before God.

On the other hand, this belief in the transference of merit was based on a true idea of the organic unity of the race. The Jewish race was bound up into one with its great progenitors; and it is these men who are its true representatives. They show what their race can be and is meant to be, and along what lines it is meant to move. Their election and walk with God laid a consecration on all who came after them; as St. Paul elsewhere says that the children of a Christian parent in a mixed marriage are holy, i.e. have a consecration laid upon them by their partly Christian parentage[15]. The patriarchs exhibit Israel as God means it to be. And God, so to speak, cannot forget that every Israelite is a child of Abraham and Isaac and Jacob, and that in their faith and religion lies his possibility and his glory.

Thus stated, the idea of the 'communion of saints' in the Jewish race is nothing else than a ground of hope, and a stimulus to recovery. And the idea admits at once of being transferred to the catholic Israel, as in fact its Jewish parody has, at certain periods, been only too fully and fatally transferred. I say, the true idea admits of being transferred. We belong to the same body as the apostles and martyrs, the virgins and saints, the Jewish patriarchs and prophets also. Their possibilities are ours. Their God is our God for ever and ever. And God looks on us as in one body with them. We too are beloved for these our fathers' sakes. And they too, we cannot doubt, are conscious of our fellowship with them, and if we are trying to live in the same spirit with them, we must believe, all the limitations of our knowledge notwithstanding, that they are supporting and helping us, as in Christ our sympathetic advocates and allies.

4. The metaphor of the olive and the grafting is intelligible enough without explanation. We know how often the olive and the vine are taken in the Old Testament and in other Jewish writings—as in the passage just quoted from the Talmud—for a symbol of Israel; we must frankly recognize that St. Paul, apparently in forgetfulness and not by design, accommodates the physical process of grafting to its spiritual counterpart; for in physical fact, of course, the ingrafted shoot (which represents the Gentiles), and not the stock upon which it is grafted (which represents the Jews), would determine the character and produce of the tree: but when this is once recognized it may be forgotten, and the metaphor is as intelligible to us as if the physical process of grafting were really as St. Paul represents it.

5. As we read the words, 'And so all Israel shall be saved,' we cannot help asking ourselves—Does St. Paul mean us to believe this of all Israelites without exception, or even of Israel in general with an absolute necessity? I think the answer should be a negative in both cases[16]. Just above St. Paul says, looking at the matter from the side of Israel, 'They also, if they continue not in unbelief, shall be grafted in.' Here he is looking at the matter from the side of God. It lies in the divine purpose that the

establishment of the catholic church, and the experience of alienation on the part of the Jews, should stimulate them to regain their ancient privileges on a new basis; 'and so,' looking at the matter from the point of view of the divine intention, 'all Israel shall be saved.' Just below, from the same point of view, it is stated to be God's purpose 'to have mercy upon all men.' But, in interpreting this latter passage, we are doing violence to what St. Paul says elsewhere with emphatic distinctness, if we imagine that he asserts that all individual men without exception shall ultimately attain the end of their being and the fellowship of God. In these passages, as elsewhere, St. Paul looks at things from two points of view, without attempting to present us with a harmony of them. From one point of view we have spread out before us the 'mystery,' or revealed secret of God, and discern the purpose of His love working on, and finding its opportunities even in the gravest moral disasters. From the other point of view we detect human wilfulness, able in a measure, but never completely or on the whole, to baffle and thwart the divine purpose. St. Paul, I say, is content to recognize both points of view, and not to hold them in complete combination. He uses the perception of the divine purpose—in this case, the recovery of the Jews—as a motive for hope and thankfulness and renewed energy; but he does not, apparently, ask himself the metaphysical questions whether God foreknows how particular individuals or groups of men will act, or, if we must say that God does so foreknow how each man will act, how this is reconcilable with his moral freedom. He is content to adore the divine purpose, and rest upon it; and recognize, on the other hand, the thwarting power of human wilfulness.

From the point of view of God's patiently loving purpose, then, a great and fresh opportunity is being prepared for the recovery of the whole of Israel, when 'the times of the Gentiles' are fulfilled and the Church stands really catholic before their eyes. Just in the same way, in the larger field of all mankind, the purpose of God is at work through all rejections, and all judgements of hardening, to convince all men of their need of God, and so prepare their hearts 'that he might have mercy upon all.' But from the other point of view God respects human freedom. Thus over against the divine purpose stands the ambiguous human 'if'—'if they continue not in their unbelief.'

This ambiguous human element is a prominent feature in Old Testament prophecy, though there too the thwarting power of man's perverseness is limited. If not in one way then in another, if not through one set of agents then through others—on the whole the purpose of God finds its sure way to accomplishment.

RETROSPECT OVER THE ARGUMENT

And now that we have given all the pains we can to entering into the spirit of these chapters, may we not say that they have become no longer repellent but deeply attractive? Where could we find a more liberating outlook over the wide purpose of God in redeeming the world? Sin is a stern fact, and demands stern dealing to overcome it by moral discipline. Men of all sorts must be brought to realize their need of God, utterly to expel the false dream of independence, and humbly to welcome the unmerited bounty of the divine 'mercy,' the free gift of pardon and new life. This then is the way in which the fundamental purpose of God for man shows itself in a world of sin; it is by a discipline preparing men to welcome a divine mercy of which they have learnt to know their need. 'That he may have mercy upon all'—this is the generous end upon which all the divine dealings with men converge. The Jews by one kind of discipline while they still were standing together as the elect people of God, and by another when, having rejected the Christ and fallen out of their religious leadership, they were to be stirred to jealousy by the spectacle of a divine fellowship from which they were excluded: the Gentiles by a different sort of discipline, and each separate race by its own; nay more, every individual, Jew and Greek, Englishman or Hindoo, by a distinctive personal chastening, in as many ways as man is various and God is resourceful: all men are so to be dealt with as that all men shall be brought to confess themselves to be as they are in God's sight, and surrender themselves to Him to be refashioned after the divine image. Through all national and personal vocations realized, by which human character is educated: through all national and personal humiliations, which are divine judgements by which human character is corrected and made docile: God's untiring patience and forbearance, in sternness and in love, works on to the one universal end—that He might have mercy upon all. The uttermost and most pitiable collapse, even the imminence of death itself, may be, nay certainly in God's intention is, His remedy for human wilfulness: a means by which—

'God unmakes but to remake the soul
He else made first in vain, which must not be[17].'

—must not be, that is, so far as the resourcefulness of divine love, going all lengths short of destroying the fundamental moral choice of the soul, can avail to prevent it. This teaching of St. Paul suggests a wonderful way of reading human history, and inspires us with the right sort of patience and hopefulness in our attitude towards the wider problems of missionary work and our own dealings with individuals. The races to whose conversion we would fain minister seem so immovable and so indifferent. The men and women whom we would fain help seem so hardened or so weak. But 'the gifts and callings of God' within them and about them, 'are without repentance.' God's remedies for them are not yet exhausted. We therefore have a right to hope and labour on, 'never despairing[18].'

And where is a nobler presentation to be found than here of the idea of divine election? That in the great household of the world there are magnificent and (comparatively, at least) ignominious vocations among races and individuals; that some men are born for the top, and other men for the bottom of society; that there are 'honourable' and 'dishonourable' limbs in the body of humanity, the latter fulfilling their necessary function no less than the former, is an indisputable fact. It is no use challenging it, any more than any other fundamental law of the universe. And, if we can see why certain races and certain individuals are fitted for certain tasks, yet on the whole we can advance but a very little way in seeing the reason of human inequalities as in fact they exist. All that lies in the inscrutable and free counsels of God, and the responsibility is—in spite of the modifying effects of human sin—ultimately His[19]. But in St. Paul's treatment of it, the recognition of the fact that God works universal ends through selected races and individuals, is robbed of all that ministers to pride and narrowness in the elect, or to hopelessness and a sense of injustice in the rest.

The New Testament writers in general would teach us that with God is no respect of persons; so that the lowest vocation may result in the highest glory, where it is faithfully fulfilled, and the highest vocation, misused, in the deepest degradation; but St. Paul in particular makes us feel the humbling responsibility which attaches necessarily to any state of election. The Jews failed because they lacked the faith and docility which would have enabled them to correspond to God's larger leading. The time came when God who had, 'through the Jews, prepared the Christ for the world,' had also, 'through the Gentiles, prepared the world for Christ'; but the Jews were ready neither to welcome the Christ, nor to 'receive' the world. Thus the richest ministry ever vouchsafed to a race was waiting for the Jews, and they proved false to it, because they had turned their privileges into an occasion for pride and selfishness, and would not learn the new truth or rise to the new opportunity.

Here is a serious warning to the 'elect' of every age. How often has the church at large, or a national church, refused the call to expansion, and lost some rich part of its heritage because it was self-satisfied, and therefore blind? How often does a 'good catholic' fail to recognize that he is utterly misusing the gifts of grace, if his Catholicism does not mean a generous and self-sacrificing desire to win the lost and save the world? How often has the profession of being 'saved' put an end to spiritual growth and the struggle with sin? How many religious orders and societies have lived on the reputation of the past, and appeared to fancy that the achievements of their founders—'the merits of the fathers'—would justify the apathy and carelessness of those who had inherited an honourable name? Indeed, to whatever we are elect—whether national, or ecclesiastical, or personal privileges—the temptation dogs us to rest on our inherited merits and have no open ear to the guiding voice of God, as it calls us to fresh ventures and renewed sacrifices, like those which laid the basis of the position of which we now make our empty or insolent boast. But thus to evade the uncomfortable requirements of the present by an appeal to the achievements of the past—whether it be the past of catholic tradition or 'the Reformation settlement'—is to expose ourselves inevitably to divine condemnation.

Those who keep the open ear are the 'remnant' in every age and church and nation. They are the men who refuse to 'make the word of God of none effect,' because of the blinding, deadening force of social tradition. They are alive and awake to 'buy up the opportunity,' as it presents itself. And for such St. Paul's teaching, inherited from the prophets, of the function of the remnant is full of encouragement. The Bible is a book contemptuous of majorities. The mass of men, conventional, easily satisfied, self-centred, accomplish nothing, redeem and regenerate nothing. But those who have ears to hear have every motive, though they be few in number, to live at the highest level possible, and believe to the full that the purpose of God can be realized. God's purpose can work, and has in history worked, through small minorities, through single individuals. They are the true representatives of their church, their nation, their class. And when the inner history of any epoch comes to be known, while the inert mass of people, 'important' or 'unimportant,' is lost in the dim background, they will be seen distinctive in the foreground: the real movement of God in history, the real witness of the truth, the real spiritual succession of the kingdom of God, will be seen to have been carried on through them for the enriching of the whole world.

I would add two reflections on subordinate, but still important points. It is the function of the catholic church to let its light so shine before men that it shall 'provoke to jealousy,' by the manifest presence of God in the midst of it, the ancient and now alienated people, the Jews. At the moment, with the anti-semite cry strong throughout Europe, and on the morrow of the 'affaire Dreyfus,' these words ring with a bitter irony. And in our own East London how utterly unlikely it is that the spectacle of our Christianity should make the Jews feel that Christian society cannot but be divine!

Indeed, the unfulfilled debt Christendom owes to the Jews is appalling. That ancient and indomitable race retains, with all its faults, its close-knitting sense of brotherhood, its faith, its frugality, its industry, its patience, its heroism. We are meant to show it the greater glories of the New Covenant, the splendour of the purity, the unworldliness, the expansiveness, the love of the brotherhood of Christ. And we do show it—what? Is there that in our common Christianity, as they see it, which should obviously make Judaism ashamed of itself? Could St. Paul, looking at our Christendom, have expected 'all Israel to be saved' by the spectacle of a catholic church? These are considerations which indeed should drive us to bitter penitence and earnest prayer.

Finally, before we leave these chapters, we shall do well to look steadily at St. Paul's habit of mind in dealing with antithetic or complementary truths. No one could believe with a more glorious conviction than St. Paul in the dominance of the purpose of God in the world: in the certainty of the accomplishment of what God has predestined. If the very rejection of the Christ by the Jews was turned into an opportunity for the conversion of the Gentiles, what crime can be too great for the divine wisdom to overrule it for good? No one, on the other hand, could realize more deeply the responsibility which lies upon men: their strange power to correspond with God, or partly thwart His purpose for them and through them. My point is only this: he is true to both sides of an antithesis, even though the exact relationship and interworking of the twin truths is necessarily and finally obscure. He refuses to be one-sided at the requirement of an incomplete human logic. It has been often pointed out, and in many directions, how prone we all are to take up with one side of truth—with predestination or free-will, with the divinity or the manhood of Christ, with the unity or the trinity of the Godhead, with sacraments or conversion, with authority or personal judgement; and if we are intellectually disposed, we call our one-sidedness 'being logical.' But we had better let St. Paul teach us once for all that impartiality is a greater thing than this cheap logic; even as Church history teaches us that a sharp-witted but one-sided zeal for truth is one main cause of bitterness, narrowness, and schism.

[1] I follow, by preference, the paragraphs of the R.V., unless there is very strong reason to the contrary.

[2] Cf. 2 Cor. v. 19, 'God was in Christ reconciling the world unto Himself.'

[3] Num. xv. 20, 21.

[4] 'The Lord called thy name A green olive tree.' Jer. xi. 16; Hos. xiv. 6.

[5] On 'mystery,' see Ephesians, p. 73. It means a divine secret disclosed to the elect.

[6] Isa. lix. 20, according to the Greek, and xxvii. 9. Cf. Ezek. xxxvi. 25, 26.

[7] Isa. xl. 13. Cf. Job xxxviii. 4; xli. 11; Wisd. ix. 13.

[8] Jer. xxxviii. 4.

[9] Ezek. xvi. 61.

[10] See above, vol. i. 3.

[11] Ezek. xxxvii.

[12] See my Ephesians, pp. 258 ff.

[13] Quoted, with much other illustrative matter, by Weber, l.c., pp. 293 ff. The fancy is based on 1 Kings xix. 36; Exod. xxxii. 13. Cf. on Cant. i. 5, 'I am black but comely'—'The congregation of Israel speaks: I am black through mine own works, but lovely through the works of my fathers.'

[14] Ezek. xiv. 14.

[15] 1 Cor. vii. 14.

[16] 'All Israel,' in 1 Kings xii. 1, 2 Chron. xii. 1, Dan. ix. 11, means 'Israel in general.'

[17] These words (which in their full sense seem to go beyond what we have a right to say) occur in Browning's Ring and the Book. It is the Pope's final reflection, when he condemns Guido to death, that his execution may be the one chance for his spiritual recovery—

'In the main criminal I see no chance
Except in such a suddenness of fate.'

[18] Luke vi. 35, or 'despairing of no man,' marg. R.V.

[19] We hold, therefore, with regard to the lots of men in this world, exactly the opposite of what Plato suggested under the impulse of the doctrine of transmigration, 'It is the man's own choice, God is blameless.'

DIVISION V. CHAPTERS XII-XV. 13.

Practical Exhortation.

We must almost all of us, in climbing some high hill, have experienced the necessity for two distinct efforts, the second more or less unanticipated. We started to climb to the apparent summit, only to find, when we got there, that it was no real summit at all, but a prominent spur, and that a second climb was required of us before we were really at the top. An intellectual experience not unlike this is the lot of the student of the Epistle to the Romans. The apparent climax of the epistle is the end of chapter viii, and the student at starting expects his brain to be chiefly taxed in following the closely knit argument which is to lead him thither. But he reaches it only to find another like effort of mind required of him in grasping the meaning of the section (chapters ix-xi) in which St. Paul is occupied in justifying God's dealings with the chosen people. But now, intellectually speaking, his work is almost over. As the climber, seated on the summit of the hill when at last it is gained, lets his eye range over a rich and wide prospect, and takes in its vastness and variety, or traces below him the delightful descent: so it is with the reader of this epistle who has entered sincerely into the spirit of St. Paul. His intellectual scruples as to the divine dealings have been just laid to rest; before that his mind had been convinced, and his heart and will attracted and won, by the unfolding of the divine righteousness, that is to say of the free grace and love of God. And now, proportionate to the greatness of the effort by which this satisfaction of intellect and heart and will has been won, is the joy of expansion which remains—the joy of the surrendered mind in appreciating all that is practically possible for it in the light of the love of God. 'I will run the way of thy commandments, because thou dost enlarge my heart,' that is, expand it with a sense of liberty and joy[1]. 'All things are ours,' if but once in completeness of self-surrendering faith 'we are Christ's' as assuredly 'Christ is God's[2].' 'I can do all things in Christ that strengtheneth me[3].'

[1] Ps. cxix. 32. See Driver's Parallel Psalter, Oxford (1898).

[2] 1 Cor. iii. 21-3.

[3] Phil. iv. 13.

DIVISION V. § I. CHAPTER XII. 1-2.

Self-surrender in response to God.

And first of all the general attitude of mind is defined, which it befits us to adopt towards God as He has now revealed Himself to us. It is the response of entire self-surrender—the response of sacrifice to sacrifice. St. Paul 'beseeches,' or rather 'encourages,' or 'summons' the Roman Christians, using for his motive power[1] all the rich store of divine compassions which he has just been occupied in disclosing or explaining to them, to make the only response really possible to such an exhibition of divine love; and that is to present themselves in sacrifice to God. What God asks is not dead victims but living men, in body as well as spirit consecrated to His service and rendered acceptable in His sight: and this sort of self-oblation, on the pattern of Christ, is the only reasonable sort of divine service for man to offer. The transitory world, to which such an ideal is quite alien, is indeed all around them, but they are not to suffer themselves to be assimilated to its fleeting fashion. Their whole point of view is changed and become new; and this must result in so thorough a transformation of their old worldly ways of thinking that a new inward light will shine in their hearts, and they will be able to discriminate and see what God's will is, and so to follow the way of perfection.

I beseech you therefore, brethren, by the mercies of God, to present your bodies a living sacrifice, holy, acceptable to God, which is your reasonable service. And be not fashioned according to this world: but be ye transformed by the renewing of your mind, that ye may prove what is the good and acceptable and perfect will of God.

This short paragraph is full of meaning, and is profoundly characteristic of St. Paul in thought and language.

The 'therefore' is one of the great transitional 'therefores[2]' by which St. Paul shows his constant sense of the inter-connexion of doctrine and life: the doctrine passing by a clear logic into the practical life, and the life drawing all its practical motives from the realities disclosed in the doctrine. It is truly nothing whatever but shallowness and 'shortness of thought' which can suffer us to imagine that the Christian character—I do not say all morality, but the Christian character—could long survive the Christian creed.

And the character of this summary exhortation shows us that any idea of a faith which stops short of moral identification with its object is utterly alien to St. Paul's mind. Faith is no true Christian faith, if it is content to receive from the Father, or from Christ, a gift which leaves it still outside the life of God. The faith which Christ inspires asks for and receives nothing less than real fellowship in His divine and human life, and that life is, in its joys as well as its sorrows, a life of self-surrender, of sacrifice. Thus the Christian only welcomes the gift of pardon through Christ's sacrifice in order to be admitted into the freedom of the dedicated life in Christ, which is the life of sacrifice. It is the sort of sacrifice (as St. Paul's language indicates) which is as different as possible from any such asceticism as is prompted by contempt of the flesh or the body, or refusal of joy, or love of death. It is sacrifice which seeks to cultivate into full vitality every faculty of body as well as of mind (and that in an active society or brotherhood), in order to consecrate all we are or can be to the service of God, and so realize in conscious correspondence with the divine will the rational worship for humanity.

St. Paul's words here about a 'living' as opposed to a bloody, and a 'rational' as opposed to an animal sacrifice, may be the basis on which the eucharist, the Christian worship 'in spirit and in truth,' was often called in early times the 'reasonable' and 'bloodless sacrifice[3].' And whether this be the case or no, at any rate we must relearn the lesson that St. Augustine is for ever insisting upon, that the eucharistic sacrifice essentially involves and implies the offering of the Church as the body of Christ, that is, the offering of ourselves as members of the body; and we may feel profoundly thankful that, in our service of Holy Communion, this truth has been restored to its proper prominence, after having been, in the pre-Reformation service, almost ignored. 'And here we offer and present unto thee, O Lord, ourselves, our souls and bodies, to be a reasonable, holy, and lively sacrifice unto thee.' In this prayer is really the climax of our sacrificial worship[4].

The true service of God is intelligent correspondence with the divine will—this is perfection; and to correspond with the divine will we must be able to know it: and this is what we can do if we are true to the principle of our new birth, and suffer it radically and permanently to transform us and our point of view (for nothing less than this is carried by St. Paul's expression rendered 'transform'). Negatively, this means that we must maintain our separateness from the worldly world, to which we died at our baptism—the world of human society as it devotes itself to its business and its pleasures, leaving God out of account[5]. For if the worldly world is suffered to fashion us in accordance with its shallow and transitory show (this is the idea conveyed by the word rendered 'fashion'), we shall be blinded to what our regeneration ought to have made plain to us.

[1] For the use of 'by,' cf. xv. 30; 1 Cor. i. 10 ('through' is the same word); 2 Cor. x. 1.

[2] See further, Ephes. pp. 172 ff.

[3] It is more likely, however, that the phrases 'rational worship' and 'bloodless sacrifice' had an earlier Jewish origin. They occur in The Testament of the XII Patriarchs, which is apparently a Jewish document christianized. There the angels are said (Levi. 3) to 'offer to the Lord a rational odour of sweet savour and a bloodless offering.' Philo also, as Mr. Conybeare points out to me, in several passages describes the true sacrifices as 'bloodless': and by bloodless sacrifices he means either the meal offerings as opposed to the animal sacrifices (De Anim. Sacrif. ed. Mangey ii. 250), or truly spiritual acts as opposed to merely outward (De Ebreitate, i. p. 370, cf. ii. 254). These two ideas run easily into one another, and the earliest uses of the expression 'bloodless sacrifice' for the eucharist have a similar ambiguity.

[4] See further, p. 179. I may be allowed to express the earnest desire that we might have liberty in our Church to read both of the Post-Communion Prayers, which seem supplementary rather than alternative to one another.

[5] See Ephes. p. 92.

DIVISION V. § 2. CHAPTER XII. 3-21.

The community spirit.

And when St. Paul, justifying himself here, as before and later on, by the special divine favour which has made him the apostle of the Gentiles[1], proceeds to develop his exhortation, it appears that with him, as with St. James[2], the form in which 'divine service' shows itself must be love of the brethren. To be called into the body of Christ—the society which is bound into one by His life and spirit—is to be called to social service, that is, to live a community life, and to cultivate the virtues which make true community life possible and healthy. Of these the first is humility, which in this connexion means the viewing oneself in all things as one truly is, as a part of a whole. Of the faith by which the whole body lives, a share, but only a share, belongs to each member—a certain measure of faith—and he must not strain beyond it. But he is diligently to make the best of his faculty, and do the work for which his special gift qualifies him, in due subordination to the welfare of the whole, whether it be inspired preaching, or ordinary teaching, or the distribution of alms, or presidency, or some other form of helping others which is his special function. Besides humility there are other virtues which make the life of a community healthy and happy, and St. Paul enumerates them, as they occur to his mind, in no defined order or completeness. There must be sincerity in love, that is in considering and seeking the real interest of others; there must be the righteous severity which keeps the moral atmosphere free from taint; there must be tenderness of feeling, which makes the community a real family of brothers; and an absence of all self-assertion, or desire for personal prominence; and thorough industry; and spiritual zeal; and devotion to God's service; and the cheerfulness which Christian hope inspires; and the ready endurance of affliction; and close application to prayer; and a love for giving whenever fellow Christians need; and an eagerness to entertain them when they are travelling—for 'the community' embraces, not one church only, but 'all the churches.'

Nay in a wider sense the community extends itself to all mankind, even those who persecute[3] them. According to his Lord's precepts, the Christian is only to bless his persecutors. Generally he is to be, in the deep, original sense, sympathetic with his fellow men everywhere in their joys and sorrows, and (to return to the Christian community) he is to seek to let it be pervaded by an impartial kindness; and, not thinking himself a superior person suited only for superior affairs, he is to let the current of ordinary human needs bear him along. He is not to set undue store on his own opinions[4]; he is utterly to banish the spirit of retaliation; he is deliberately to plan so to live as that his life shall prove, not a stumblingblock, but a moral attraction to men in general[5]; he is never to quarrel with any one if he can possibly help it; he is completely to suppress his resentment when he is wronged, and simply to leave the matter to the wrath of God, as indeed the law would have him do[6]; so that, by his very meekness and returning good for evil, he may, according to the wise man's saying, heap burning shame upon his enemy, like coals of fire[7]. Evil is all around the Christian, and it is a strong man armed; but the Christian has with him the forces of good which are yet stronger, and by no passive withdrawal, but by the active exercise of good, he is to win the victory over evil.

For I say, through the grace that was given me, to every man that is among you, not to think of himself more highly than he ought to think; but so to think as to think soberly, according as God hath dealt to each man a measure of faith. For even as we have many members in one body, and all the members have not the same office: so we, who are many, are one body in Christ, and severally members one of another. And having gifts differing according to the grace that was given to us, whether prophecy, let us prophesy according to the proportion of our faith; or ministry, let us give ourselves to our ministry; or he that teacheth, to his teaching; or he that exhorteth, to his exhorting: he that giveth, let him do it with liberality; he that ruleth, with diligence; he that sheweth mercy, with cheerfulness. Let love be without hypocrisy. Abhor that which is evil; cleave to that which is good. In love of the brethren be tenderly affectioned one to another; in honour preferring one another; in diligence not slothful; fervent in spirit; serving the Lord; rejoicing in hope; patient in tribulation; continuing stedfastly in prayer; communicating to the necessities of the saints; given to hospitality. Bless them that persecute you; bless, and curse not. Rejoice with them that rejoice; weep with them that weep. Be of the same mind one toward another. Set not your mind on high things, but condescend to things that are lowly. Be not wise in your own conceits. Render to no man evil for evil. Take thought for things honourable in the sight of all men. If it be possible, as much as in you lieth, be at peace with all men. Avenge not yourselves, beloved, but give place unto wrath: for it is written, Vengeance belongeth unto me; I will recompense, saith the Lord. But if thine enemy hunger, feed him; if he thirst, give him to drink: for in so doing thou shall heap coals of fire upon his head. Be not overcome of evil, but overcome evil with good.

(1) It is the idea of corporate life which dominates all this exhortation. No writing in the New Testament has done more than the Epistle to the Romans to strengthen the sense of spiritual individuality, and to rouse the individual spirit to protest, as it protested in Luther, against spiritual

tyranny. But it is a complete mistake to suppose that the epistle is individualistic in tendency. The life into which the individual's faith in Jesus admits him is the life of a community, and its virtues are the virtues of community life. The strengthened individuality is to go to enrich an organized society.

This is expressed in the familiar metaphor of the body which had been employed in non-Christian thought before St. Paul identified it with himself and Christianity by the vigorous and profound use which he made of it[8]. The Christian community is a body bound together in a common life by a common inspiring presence and spirit. The divine grace and good favour of Christ shows itself in special 'gifts' (in the Greek this word 'charisma' expresses a particular embodiment of the general grace, 'charis,' of God); and no individual member is without his special endowment. It is not a few officers of the community who are gifted, but all; and all are to co-operate in the common life and work. Of gifts there are various sorts which we hear of in the New Testament. There are the official gifts, the result of what we call ordination, as the gift which was 'in' Timothy 'by the laying on of hands.' And those among the Christians at Rome, who 'presided' and 'ministered,' would have been, we should suppose, official presbyters or 'bishops,' and deacons. But the Roman Christians hardly constituted yet an organized church, and we cannot tell whence such officers of the community received their appointment. There is no ground for a positive assertion of any kind[9]. Again we hear of special gifts, such as powers of healing, speaking with tongues and prophesying, which sometimes accompanied the bestowal of the Spirit, through the laying on of hands which was given to all. And the gift of prophesying among the Roman Christians may have been a gift of this kind. But St. Paul is perhaps writing with the circumstances of the Corinthian church, rather than those of the Roman Christians, in his mind; and we can gather but little about the exact condition of things at the capital. Once more, St. Paul uses the word 'gifts' for more personal and moral endowments, as for the bent of mind which leads men, under divine guidance, towards celibacy or marriage[10]. But in this place he is not distinguishing. He is hardly speaking in view of any special circumstances at Rome. He is but emphasizing the fact which is the basis of all the life of Christians everywhere—the fact that each individual member of the body has a special gift, and a special function for the good of the whole body, by which the gift is to express itself. What every individual Christian has to do, then, is to realize his own gift and correspond to it. The gift involves a certain 'measure of faith.' The faith of each individual Christian is the same in its basis. It holds him in spiritual allegiance to the same Lord, and in confession of the same elemental creed. But, besides this, it involves a special insight, which is the peculiar endowment of the individual. There is something which each man can realize and impart, as no one else is qualified to do. The Church is the poorer if he holds back or fails to stir up this gift of his own, and on the other hand he incurs the peril of presumption if he ventures beyond it. Even the inspired man, the prophet, must prophesy within the limits of what his own special proportion of faith enables him to perceive and grasp[11], even though another prophet with a larger faith might rightly say what he may not venture upon. 'Let each man be fully persuaded in his own mind.' For any assertion which goes beyond what the faith of the individual enables him to be convinced of, is for him 'sin.' We greatly need this exhortation to-day. The convictions of many are vague and uncertain, and their teaching without heart or force, because, like parrots, they catch up and repeat what others may have insight enough to warrant their asserting, but they have not. To correspond with one's own personal gift of faith is to realize one's vocation; and, by the development of the individual points of view, inside the common 'tradition,' the fullness and richness of the corporate faith is secured.

The cohesion of the body lies in each one's realizing his own gift, and also reverencing that of others. Here is humility. Humility is not self-contempt, or cringing to others. To realize one's own gift, one's own relation to God, gives to each man a dignity, a power to stand upright and face the world. The sovereign Master and Giver has given me my own life and my own gifts. He is responsible for the existence which He gave me, and I am not to shame Him by shrinking from making the best of it. But also humility is, in all relations, truth about ourselves. It is truth about ourselves as regards God, who is simply the giver of whatever we have and are; and it is truth about ourselves as regards our fellow men—our own gifts being justly appraised only when they are regarded as means of serving the body as a whole, without any self-aggrandizement, with a due respect to the gifts of others, and even a positive will to let them have higher place than ourselves.

Indeed we shall do well to meditate deeply on this. What good work is there which is not in more or less continual danger of suffering, or even being abandoned, because fellow Christians, zealous fellow Christians, will plainly, and it must be wilfully, yield to the ambition to be first: will not be content to be second or third: will not do the unobtrusive work: will think 'How can I shine,' rather than 'How can I serve'? In fact, how very unwilling we are to recognize, in our ideals of education, and in our theory of grown life, that ambition, in the strict sense of the word—the desire to obtain distinction for ourselves, as distinct from the desire to serve—is not a motive which Christianity can sanction, or from which it can hope for a blessing.

We linger lovingly, wistfully, on the picture of the corporate life of a Christian community. Has it vanished from the earth, this real fraternal living, 'high and low, rich and poor, one with another,' each supplementing the deficiencies of the other, and receiving of their fullness? May we not do something more than we are doing to realize it in our congregations or parishes? Is nearly enough emphasis laid on the social relationship of each congregation of fellow worshippers or each local church?

Dimly through the mist of ages in old churchwardens' accounts, in the rare instances where they have been preserved from days before the Reformation, we discern what a really fraternal, self-governing and mutually co-operative community the mediaeval English parish was. Let me extract a few sentences from the excellent preface[12] which Bishop Hobhouse prefixed to an edition of the surviving Churchwardens' Accounts of a number of Somersetshire parishes.

'The (parish) community was completely organized with a constitution which recognized the rights of the whole and of every adult member to a voice in self-government, but kept the self-governing community under a system of inspection and (if need should be) restraint from central authority.' 'The whole adult population were accounted parishioners, and had an equal voice when assembled for consultation under the rector. Seeing that both sexes served the office of warden, there can be no doubt that both had a vote.'

The strongly existing spirit of good will and pride in the parish church found all the necessary funds for the maintaining of the church and the services, and for the provision of often a sumptuous and rich treasury of ornaments. The needs of the Church were met generally by the local industry of 'such as were wise-hearted'—builders, carpenters, workers in gold and silver, bell-founders, embroiderers, writers, illuminators, bookbinders, and others.

Hard by the church the church-house was the centre of the popular recreations of the holy day or holiday.

The parish elected and paid its own officers, except the rector, and the affairs and ornaments of the church, even in part the arrangement of the services, were under the government, not of the rector, but of the parish meeting, of which he was president, under the restraining hand of the rural dean and archdeacon.

The support of the poor or disabled was a wholly voluntary matter. 'The brotherhood tie was so strongly realized by the community, that the weaker ones were succoured by the stronger as out of a family store.'

'All the tendency of the feudal system, working through the machinery of the manorial court, was to keep the people down. All the tendency of the parochial system, working through the parish council, holding its assemblies in the churches, where the people met on equal terms as children and servants of the living God, and members of one body in Christ Jesus, was to lift the people up.' In these assemblies there was no distinction between lord and vassal, high and low, rich and poor; in them the people learnt the worth of being free. Here were the schools in which, in the slow course of centuries, they were disciplined to self-help, self-reliance and self-respect[13].

No doubt these descriptions of mediaeval parish life represent an ideal very imperfectly realized. But is it not an ideal we need to recover? Is there not a call for Church reform, both moral and formal, to restore to us the community life of our parishes, and fill St. Paul's language again with its primary and natural meaning?

[1] See i. 5, 11-15; xv. 15-17.

[2] Jas. i. 17.

[3] The word is the same as St. Paul has just used to describe the eager 'pursuit' of opportunities of hospitality by the Christian. He 'pursues' opportunities of doing good, while he is himself 'pursued' by enemies to do him evil.

[4] Cf. xi. 25, and Prov. iii. 7.

[5] Prov. iii. 4 LXX. 'Provide things honourable in the sight of the Lord and of man.'

[6] Deut. xxxii. 35.

[7] Prov. xxv. 21.

[8] The truth, however, which underlies the metaphor of the body is, we may say, equally present in all the New Testament writers.

[9] See, however, p. 196.

[10] 1 Cor. vii. 7.

[11] Dr. Liddon, with many others, interprets 'according to the proportion of the faith,' i.e. according to 'the majestic proportion of the (objective) faith.' This is the characteristically Latin, as against the Greek, interpretation, and the Greek is certainly to be preferred, because 'according to the proportion of our faith' follows naturally upon 'according as ... the measure of faith' just above; indeed 'faith' in this context can hardly have assigned to it without violence the objective meaning which,

however, in the context of the Pastoral Epistles it no doubt frequently bears. Cf. app. note A, p. 205.

[12] Somersetshire Records, vol. iv, 1890.

[13] Dr. Jessop, 'Parish Life in England before the Great Pillage,' Nineteenth Century, Jan. 1898, p. 55; cf. also Dom Gasquet on 'The Layman in the Mediaeval Period,' Tablet, Sept. 2, 1899.

DIVISION V. § 3. CHAPTER XIII. 1-7.

The Christians and the imperial power.

It is possible that the thought of the innocent victim of injustice and wrong waiting upon the divine wrath, brings to St. Paul's mind the idea of the State which exists to represent divine justice in the world, and minister divine wrath on behalf of the innocent. But, whether this particular connexion of thought was really in St. Paul's mind or no, at any rate the previous section has made it plain that the 'love of the brethren' must extend itself to become a right relation to all men, whether Christians or not[1]. In particular, therefore, the relation of the Christians to the imperial authority could not fail to be a matter which required attention and apostolic counsel. The Jews, whose theocratic principles made submission to government by 'the uncircumcised' at least a real abandonment of a religious ideal[2], had always an instinctive tendency to rebellion; and the Christian church built upon Judaism might easily have inherited this instinct. The catholic church of the new covenant, might have claimed to be a theocracy like that of the old. Especially at Rome, where the Jews were a vast and formidable body who had recently given trouble and been expelled[3], the attitude of the Christians, who were identified with them, might easily be misunderstood. Or on the other hand the Jews themselves, at Rome as at Thessalonica[4], might represent the Christians as disloyal to Caesar. Moreover, apart from all unjustified slanders, the spirit of the 'fifth monarchy men' has seldom been altogether absent from periods of Christian enthusiasm; and the restless and undisciplined tendencies at Thessalonica[5], which the mistaken expectation of the immediate second coming of Christ had encouraged, were a sign that Christians might easily find it difficult to settle down as good citizens in the great empire of the world.

St. Paul therefore, here and elsewhere, would make it quite plain that the catholic church, if it is like the ancient Israel, is like it only as it was in exile—when the children of Israel were bidden to be good citizens of the Babylonian empire, and to seek the peace of the city whither God had caused them to be carried away captive, and to pray unto the Lord for it, for in the peace thereof they should have peace[6]. Thus the Church was not a theocracy, but a 'settlement of strangers and exiles[7],' waiting for the visible establishment of the kingdom or city of God, and meanwhile maintaining a polity or ordered social life of their own, but on a voluntary and catholic (or non-national) basis. Therefore, so long as God maintains 'the present world,' they must be good citizens of whatever earthly state they happen to live under. On this basis, then, St. Paul reminds each single person of the duty of political loyalty. The earthly state is of God's establishing, as well as the kingdom of Christ, and fulfils a divine purpose with divine authority. It exists to suppress moral outrage and lawlessness[8], to maintain justice and right. Its officers are God's ministers (as truly as the officers of the Church, though in a different order), and must be obeyed accordingly, under peril not only of civil punishment for disobedience, but under peril of divine judgement also, and as a matter of conscience. The good man, and therefore the good Christian, has nothing to fear from the empire or its officers. And he will readily, and as a matter of conscience, pay his tribute as a subject, and his taxes as a citizen, to the proper authorities, and give to each imperial officer the respect which is his due.

Let every soul be in subjection to the higher powers: for there is no power but of God; and the powers that be are ordained of God. Therefore he that resisteth the power, withstandeth the ordinance of God: and they that withstand shall receive to themselves judgement. For rulers are not a terror to the good work, but to the evil. And wouldest thou have no fear of the power? do that which is good, and thou shalt have praise from the same: for he is a minister of God to thee for good. But if thou do that which is evil, be afraid; for he beareth not the sword in vain: for he is a minister of God, an avenger for wrath to him that doeth evil. Wherefore ye must needs be in subjection, not only because of the wrath, but also for conscience sake. For for this cause ye pay tribute also; for they are ministers of God's service, attending continually upon this very thing. Render to all their dues: tribute to whom tribute is due; custom to whom custom; fear to whom fear; honour to whom honour.

Our Lord, by His whole bearing towards Jewish nationalism and by His clear prophecy of the destruction of Jerusalem, as well as by His particular injunction to 'render unto Caesar the things that were Caesar's,' had made it evident to His disciples that the sceptre had departed from Judah, and had determined the attitude of Christians towards the empire. They could not indeed be as other inhabitants of the empire, for they were waiting, and praying, and working, for the visible establishment of a city and kingdom of God on earth—little as either the 'times and seasons,' or the character and manner, of that city and kingdom had been revealed to them. Thus the Roman empire could not but be in their eyes a kingdom of this world destined for overthrow. But it was by the methods of meekness, and by purely spiritual weapons, that the kingdom of God was to come, and the great overthrow, whatever it should prove to be, was to be effected. This at least was certain; and meanwhile the Roman empire represented the divine principle of authority and order, and must be obeyed.

St. Paul no doubt had, more than any other apostle, a real feeling for the empire and the city of which he was a citizen. Moreover, he saw in the organization of the empire a great framework and vehicle for the establishment and spread of the catholic church. And hitherto certainly (at least, since the fatal moment of Pilate's weakness) the Church had continually experienced the assistance of the imperial authorities. It was a misused spiritual authority, before which the protest had to be made, 'We must obey God rather than man[9].' It was the Jewish authorities who persecuted the Church. It was the Jewish king who put James to death. At Paphos, Thessalonica, Corinth, Ephesus, the imperial authorities had been more or less friendly, and even at Philippi they had been reduced to an attitude of apology by the bare mention of Roman citizenship. St. Paul's experiences, therefore, had prepared him to 'appeal unto Caesar,' and to expect justice and freedom for himself and his cause. Even the beginnings of the experience of imperial hostility and persecution did not quash or even weaken this attitude in St. Peter[10]. St. Peter and St. Paul idealize the empire almost as if it could do no wrong, and the righteous had nothing to fear from it. Of course, when this expectation had been rudely shattered—when the imperial authority had come chiefly to mean the persecution of the saints—an opposite sort of idealism takes place, and Rome appears as the great 'beast' of violence in the Apocalypse of John. Both idealizations represent truth—the truth of what the State is meant to be on the one side, and of what it may become on the other. But after considerable experience of persecution, Clement of Rome is still full of admiration for the divine order of the imperial rule, and recognizes the duty of obedience to his 'rulers and governors upon earth,' side by side with the duty of obedience to 'God's almighty and most excellent name'; and as it is God who has given the rulers their authority, he prays for grace to submit to them, and offers rich prayer for their welfare and that of the empire. And the spirit lived on in the Christian church through all the persecutions, and the apologists for Christianity loved to protest their loyalty to the empire, and to think of their church as 'the soul of the world,' maintaining it by prayer and virtue in the midst of impiety and corruption.

In England this passage has often been put to two conspicuously unjustifiable uses. First, it was the stronghold of the maintainers of 'the divine right of kings' and of 'passive obedience.' In reality it asserts the divine right of civil authority, but not of any particular kind of civil authority. Indeed the government of the empire was still nominally a republic in its fundamental forms, though it was becoming a despotism in fact. And supposing the senate and people had—as is of course conceivable—reasserted their authority over their 'emperors,' or military officers, the Christian doctrine of divine right would have afforded no guidance as to which of the claimants to authority had the divine will on its side. What is barely asserted is the divine right of the existing civil authority, democratic or regal. And while our passage exalts the normal duty of obedience, it suggests no answer to the question—Is there not a point where a government so manifestly fails to maintain the divine order in the world, or to represent the will of God and the best interests of the people, that it deserves to be put an end to? At such a point Christianity can only serve to reinforce the natural instincts of justice and right.

And again, the words, 'the powers that be are ordained of God: therefore he that resisteth the power withstandeth the ordinance of God,' have often been used in England to justify a claim on behalf of the State to coerce and govern the Church and the consciences of men in spiritual matters. But such an idea is utterly alien to the mind of the New Testament. In the matters which concern our spiritual salvation, the authority which is to discipline and control us is the binding and loosing, absolving and retaining, authority which is entrusted not to the State, but to the Church. Attempts are recorded in history on the part of the State to crush out the Church, and on the part of the Church to usurp the authority of the State and use its weapons. Such attempts, we trust, belong to past history. An attempt, too, specially identified with England, has been made to identify a national Church and State as only different aspects of the same society, so that the government of the national Church can be more or less fused in that of the State. But whatever may be said of such an attempt in the past, in our modern England the plain facts of the political and religious situation are flatly repugnant to it; and there can evidently be no reasonable religious government in the Church of England till it is conducted again in obedience to the fundamental Christian principle that our national and local Church is part of a great catholic society, which Christ endowed with an independent spiritual authority, and a law and constitution and ministers of its own. The State may need an established national church as much as ever to enable it to fulfil its highest functions, but any 'Establishment' in these days must be consistent with the fullest recognition of the spiritual and political liberties of those members of the State who belong to other religious bodies, and also must be based upon recognition that the Church and State are fundamentally distinct, and relatively independent societies.

But it behoves us Churchmen, not only to assert the spiritual liberties of the Church, but also to realize a great deal more fully than we do, the divine authority of the civil ministers and civil laws in their own department. The State exists to embody and represent in the world the divine justice, which is to be the basis of the government of men. Its ministers—magistrates, legislators, officers of justice—are 'God's ministers': laws which are passed by the State in fulfilment of its divine mission—laws intended to maintain the health and prosperity of the people as a whole—have a divine sanction;

and we Churchmen can only be what the Church should be, 'the soul of the world,' if we make it a matter of conscience, a great deal more deliberately than it is at present with most of us, to aid vigorously in the administration of the good laws which already exist, national and municipal, and to promote intelligently and enthusiastically the purposes of civil government by helping towards better laws; so that our government, as a whole, may become a continually completer image of the equitable and impartial righteousness of God.

[1] Cf. 2 Pet. i. 7, 'In your love of the brethren supply love,' i.e. let the temper bred inside the closer bond of Christian fellowship extend itself universally.

[2] Deut. xvii. 15, 'Thou mayest not put a foreigner over thee, which is not thy brother.'

[3] Acts xviii. 2. 'Claudius had commanded all the Jews to depart from Rome,' cf. Suetonius, Claud. 25. 'The Jews who had been persistently breaking into disturbances at the instigation of Chrestus (Christ?) he expelled from Rome.' We cannot certainly explain these words, but St. Paul knew all about the occurrence from Priscilla and Aquila, whom the expulsion had brought across his path at Corinth.

[4] Acts xvii. 7.

[5] 1 Thess. iv. 11; v. 14; 2 Thess. iii. 6.

[6] Jer. xxix. 7; cf. 1 Tim. ii. 2.

[7] 1 Pet. i. 11. The word for such a 'settlement of strangers,' paroecia, has become, by a suggestive history, our 'parish.'

[8] Cf. 2 Thess. ii. 6. 'That which restraineth' the outbreak of lawlessness is (almost certainly) the empire, and 'he that restraineth' (ver. 7) the emperor.

[9] Acts v. 29.

[10] 1 Pet. ii. 13-17.

DIVISION V. § 4. CHAPTER XIII. 8-10.

The summary debt.

Christians are willingly to pay tribute and tax as a debt, a thing due in God's sight to His ministers. But this obligation is a specimen of innumerable obligations which we owe to our 'neighbours'—debts only limited by human need. And the Christian is to take a wide view of his obligations, and to let there be no legitimate claim upon him unfulfilled, no debt unpaid, except the one which a man ought always to be paying and still to be owing, for it is infinite—the debt of love. Here, in loving each other man with the same real regard to his personal interests as we devote to our own, is the satisfaction of the moral law. All the particular 'commandments'—those of the Second Table, and any other there may be—are comprehended in this one. For love can do no harm to any other, and can therefore break no commandment.

Owe no man anything, save to love one another: for he that loveth his neighbour hath fulfilled the law. For this, Thou shalt not commit adultery, Thou shall not kill, Thou shalt not steal, Thou shalt not covet, and if there be any other commandment, it is summed up in this word, namely, Thou shalt love thy neighbour as thyself. Love worketh no ill to his neighbour: love therefore is the fulfilment of the law.

St. Paul gives here a very noticeable expansion to the idea of not being in debt. In its literal sense we have all of us a horror of it, at least in theory.

'No debtor's hands are clean
However white they be.'

We must both let that theoretic horror of debt dominate our practice in money matters, and also expand our idea of 'debts.' According to Christ's teaching, the priest and Levite did not pay their debt to their Samaritan neighbour, because they thought him a stranger with no claim on them. Dives ignored his rich man's debt to Lazarus. Of those who are to appear on the left hand of Christ's judgement-seat, each will be condemned because he never realized his debt to Christ in the persons of all those who had needs to which he might have ministered. St. Paul, as an apostle, acknowledged his debt to all the Gentile world[1], and we members of a church, catholic in idea, but as yet so far from catholic in fact—we Englishmen, members of an imperial and spreading race, responsible for the name of Christ all over the world—have a portentous and lamentably unfulfilled debt to the races of Africa and India, and to the whole world.

We can all think of manifold debts—to the lonely whom we might visit, the misunderstood whom we might sympathize with, the ignorant whom we might teach, the weak and oppressed whom we might support and combine, the sinful whom we might convert and establish in good living; so many debts to family and friends; so many debts to Englishmen and fellow Christians, to Africans and Asiatics. Is it not bewildering even to attempt to realize our debts? And yet, let a man make a beginning, and all will be well. Let him steadily set himself to behave towards those whom he employs or those who employ him, towards his domestic servants or his masters, towards railway porters and shop assistants and others who minister to his convenience, as being men and women with the same right to courteous treatment, and to a real opportunity to make the best of themselves, as he has himself; let him steadily refuse to 'exploit' those immediately concerned with him, or treat them as merely means to his ends or instruments of his convenience; let him thus realize his debts to his nearest 'neighbours,' and the whole idea of humanity, of brotherhood, will be deepened and made real to him. Serving the few, he will come to serve the many. His prayers will go before his actions, and enlarge their scope. He will get a habit of considerateness and thoughtfulness for others, as belonging to Christ, which will express itself habitually towards all, and especially the weak. His 'neighbour' will come to mean, as in our Lord's parable and in St. Paul's expression in this place, any 'other man[2].' And in our days when the old personal relations of masters to workers have been so largely merged in the relation of companies to unions or to men and women in masses, we shall never allow ourselves to forget that combinations are combinations of individuals, and that neither individual responsibility, nor responsibility for the individual, can be obliterated by union or by numbers.

St. Paul, we notice, is here plainly reproducing our Lord's saying about love and the law[3]; and he would seem to have the teaching of the parable about the Good Samaritan in his mind; as in the previous section the saying 'Render unto Caesar the things that are Caesar's,' and in the end of the preceding one (xii. 14, 19) the prohibition of vengeance and the injunction of love to enemies in the Sermon on the Mount. St. Paul's ethical teaching is in fact found to be throughout based on our Lord's, whether our Lord's words were with him in a written form or came to him simply in the oral tradition.

And we do well to remember, as we read this familiar passage, that here is the centre and kernel of Christianity. It is the revelation of a new and universal duty, based on a revealed relationship of all men to a common Father: the duty which lies upon all men of loving all men, because God loves all men with a father's love, or rather because God is love, and only by the life of love can we share His fellowship[4]. The Christian 'enthusiasm for humanity' has thus its roots in a disclosure of the character of God, and of His mind towards every man.

[1] Rom. i. 14.

[2] ver. 8, 'his neighbours': margin, 'the other.'

[3] Matt. xxii. 40; cf. Gal. v. 14, and James ii. 8.

[4] It has been commonly said that Christianity almost created a new word to express the new duty. But this now appears not to be strictly the case. Agape, love, is a word unknown indeed to classical writers, but it is found in the popular speech of Alexandria in the second century B.C. See Deissmann, Bibelstudien (Marburg, 1895), p. 80. (I was referred to this work by Dr. Bernard, Pastoral Epistles, p. 24.) Hence, i.e. from the popular speech of Greek Egypt, it passed into the Greek Bible and so into Christianity.

DIVISION V. § 5. CHAPTER XIII. 11-14.

The approach of the day.

And the motive for paying our debts, in this wide sense, is that we must 'agree with our adversary quickly, while we are with him in the way,' for the day of account is at hand. This worldly world lies asleep to the spiritual realities, but its short night—the time of darkness—is nearly over. The great deliverance is nearer to us than when we first became Christians. The day of the Lord is almost dawning. Let us see to it then that all that is only fit for the darkness is stripped off us: that we are suitably equipped for the day, so that when it suddenly dawns it shall not put us to shame. Sensual lusts and loveless passions indulged—gross sins, such as none of the Christian communities had quite got rid of—will appear improper conduct indeed when the sun rises. And there is only one garment proper for the day; it is the garment of Christ's righteousness, or rather of Christ Himself, with whom we must invest ourselves. As for our lower nature, it is to be our servant merely—not a master, whose clamorous demands we are to study to satisfy.

'And this, knowing the season, that now it is high time for you to awake out of sleep: for now is salvation nearer to us than when we first believed. The night is far spent, and the day is at hand: let us therefore cast off the works of darkness, and let us put on the armour of light. Let us walk honestly, as in the day; not in revelling and drunkenness, not in chambering and wantonness, not in strife and jealousy. But put ye on the Lord Jesus Christ, and make not provision for the flesh, to fulfil the lusts thereof.

St. Paul, no doubt, was still in eager expectation of the immediate second coming of Christ; and that expectation has proved mistaken. Now our Lord plainly did not mean His disciples to know when His judgement was to be made manifest, and St. Paul apparently recognized this[1], so that his immediate anticipation of the end can never have been part of his faith—never more than the reflection of the eager desire which filled the heart of the Church. On the other hand, our Lord did mean His disciples to go on expecting Him. Thus St. Paul's admonition is as applicable now as ever. The future of the world and of each nation and institution is precarious: things which seem solid and strong may crumble and melt; how soon God is to make plain His judgements, in part or on the whole, we do not know; when each one of us is to pass by death to the great account we do not know. There is no reasonable attitude towards the unknown coming of judgement except to be ready, and, though the darkness of the alienated and godless world is all around us, to live as children of the light eagerly expecting the dawning of the day[2].

And to meet Christ we must be like Christ. And to be like Christ we must be in Christ, clothed with His righteousness, invested with His new nature, fighting with the weapons of His victorious manhood. The 'evil' which is in ourselves, the unregulated flesh, we can only 'overcome with good'—the good which is Jesus Himself: for it is no longer we that live in our bare selves, but Christ that liveth in us. We are baptized into Him, we possess His spirit, we eat His flesh and drink His blood. What remains is practically to clothe ourselves in Him[3], appropriating and drawing out into ourselves by acts of our will His very present help in trouble. So can we become like Him, and be fitted to see Him as He is[4].

This passage played a memorable part in St. Augustine's life; for when the child's voice had bidden him 'open and read,' these were the words upon which he opened, and which sealed his conversion to the faith he served so nobly—'not in rioting and drunkenness, ... but put ye on the Lord Jesus Christ.' 'I had no wish,' he tells us, 'to read any further, nor was there any need. For immediately at the end of this sentence, as if a light of certainty had been poured into my heart, all the shadows of doubt were scattered[5].'

[1] 1 Thess. v. 1: 'The day of the Lord so cometh as a thief in the night.' To know this is to have answer enough to questions about the times and seasons of the coming (v. 1).

[2] It is interesting to compare this passage with the closely similar one of Thess. v. 1-4. Cf. Eph. v. 14 ff.; vi. 11.

[3] Christ is 'put on' in baptism by all, Gal. iii. 27; but we all still need to appropriate what we have received, and so 'put Him on' for ourselves; cf. Eph. iv. 24; Col. iii. 12.

[4] See app. note G, p. 238, for an admirable prayer by Jeremy Taylor based on this thought.

[5] Conf. viii. 12.

DIVISION V. § 6. CHAPTER XIV. 1-23.

Mutual toleration.

St. Paul's practical exhortations show no definite scheme, but flow out of one another in a natural sequence. He began with the fundamental moral disposition required by life in the Christian community (xii). He proceeded to the relation between the Christian community and the government of the world outside (xiii. 1-7). This led him to lay brief and vigorous emphasis upon the universal range of Christian obligation (8-10), and the motive which is to make Christians zealous in rising to its fulfilment (11-14). Now[1] he comes back to the difficulties which arise among Christians—the difficulties in actually living together as members of the same community—difficulties on those small points of religious observance which seem so unimportant in the abstract, and which, in the actual experience of intercourse, prove to be so terribly important, and so easily give rise to a 'crisis in the Church.' How were the reasonably-minded majority[2], who thought that all kinds of food were morally indifferent, to behave towards the scrupulous who would only eat vegetables? How were those Christians, who recognized no distinction between one day and another, to behave towards people who still held the mind of the writer of Ecclesiasticus, that 'some days God had exalted and hallowed, and some he had made ordinary days[3]'?

The problem of 'lawful meats' had often been before the early Christians. It could not but have been so, seeing that those among them, who had passed under Jewish influences had been brought under a system in which the distinction between clean and unclean meats had been rigorously observed. True, our Lord had 'made all meats clean[4],' as He had opened the kingdom of heaven to all believers. And the vision which reassured St. Peter on the latter point, and forbade him 'to call any man common or unclean[5],' was expressed in a form which implied that the same principle would apply to food. But this fundamental catholic principle, in its sharp opposition to Jewish particularism, was not accepted without a struggle at every point. How hotly, for a time, the struggle raged, we dimly perceive in the narrative of the Acts, and especially in St. Paul's Epistle to the Galatians[6]. But at the Jerusalem conference the fundamental catholic principle was unmistakably reaffirmed. Gentiles were to be admitted to brotherhood without circumcision or the keeping of the law. Henceforth then the reactionaries had no ground to stand on. The law of clean and unclean meats had gone with the rest of the Jewish laws. But while the Gentiles won a complete victory on the main principle, they were required by the apostolic council to make concessions to Jewish habits in eating, such as could not affect the main principle. They were to eat meat killed in the Jewish manner, with the blood thoroughly drained out. This in itself would probably exclude them from the Gentile shambles, where also much of the meat which was for sale would have been offered to idols[7]. By the observance of such a concession, then, Jew and Gentile were to live and eat together in peace.

The actual enactment of the Jerusalem conference had a limited application to the Gentile Christians of Antioch and Syria and Cilicia[8]. But the principle was a vital and universal one: to hold firm the catholic or 'indifferentist' principle, but to make concessions for love's sake and to facilitate mutual fellowship. And this same principle St. Paul soon had reason to apply again at Corinth. There the problem was not—How could Jew and Gentile live and eat together? but How far could Gentiles, who had become Christians, associate with Gentiles who were still adherents of the old religion, and eat their meats? St. Paul, in answering this question for the Corinthians, strongly asserts the indifferentist principle—that meat of all kinds is God's gift and good, and that it can have contracted no moral pollution through any idolatrous ceremony to which it has been subjected. No questions, therefore, are to be asked as to its antecedents. In this physical sense meats which had been offered to idols might be freely eaten. But when such eating could do harm, when, for instance, one man points out to another that a particular portion of food has been part of a sacrifice, and it is plain he will be scandalized by the eating of it, then the other must abstain[9], restricting his own lawful liberty for charity and Christian brotherhood's sake.

Now St. Paul had heard of a new form of the old difficulty at Rome[10]. There was a Jewish asceticism—similar to what is found frequently among orientals, and was practised in Europe among the Pythagoreans—which required men to abstain from animal food altogether and from wine. Such was probably the rule of the Essenes in Palestine[11], as of the Therapeutae in Egypt, and such was, according to a very early authority, the rule of St. James, the Lord's brother. Such a practice, then, had found favour among a minority of Christians at Rome. And St. Paul in the passage we are now to study, in principle plainly approves of the indifferentist practice of the majority. He knows, and is persuaded in the Lord Jesus, that nothing is unclean of itself. It is, he implies, a weak and unduly scrupulous conscience which makes men vegetarians. But, on the other hand, this weaker brother—this man with less clear perception of Christian principle in the matter—must in no way be alienated. He is to be made welcome. There is no obligation upon him to eat meat. God laid no such requirement upon him when he became a Christian. 'God received him.' The Church must continue the like liberality, and not even seek to pronounce judgement in the matter. In life and death each man is Christ's servant, and is responsible to God for what he does or does not do. Therefore let each man simply be faithful to his own conscience before God in this matter, so that whatever he eats he can 'say his grace,' or 'give thanks,' with a good conscience; and let him be respectfully tolerant of his brother's practice—the strong not despising the weak, nor the weak judging and condemning the strong.

So far for liberty. But if, by using our liberty to eat meat, we are found to run a risk of really troubling our brother, or even (what is worse) leading him to act against his conscience and eat what he feels he ought not[12], then we must abstain. This becomes matter of character and peaceable fellowship and spiritual joy, and these are the really material things in the kingdom of God. Sooner than do injury to this really divine cause, sooner than be a hindrance to his brother, the Christian had better willingly abstain altogether from flesh and wine too.

In passing St. Paul had noticed another indifferent matter besides the eating of meats. It was the observance of days. St. Paul undoubtedly considered that all distinction of high days and common days, all distinction of the sabbath from other days, had been in principle abolished by Christianity. For Gentile Christians, like the Galatians, to be 'observing (Jewish) days, and months, and seasons, and years[13],' is to show a miserable disposition to fall back upon a superannuated legal idea of religion—to fall back from the religion of the Spirit to the religion of the letter; from the substance to the shadow. For the Christian, in fundamental principle, there are no 'sacred days,' for all days are indifferently sacred. As instructed Christian men could eat all meats, so they could regard all days as on the same level in God's sight. But all Christians had not the full perception of principle. Among the Galatians, indeed, the tendency to observe days is viewed more severely as part of a general reactionary tendency. But at Rome it appears to have represented simply the practice of a harmless, if imperfectly enlightened, minority, and St. Paul merely ranks it among things indifferent, which are to be frankly tolerated. It is to be purely left to the individual conscience.

With these preliminary explanations—which in this case will serve our purpose better than an analysis—we can read this section without experiencing any great difficulty.

But him that is weak in faith receive ye, yet not to doubtful disputations[14]. One man hath faith to eat all things: but he that is weak eateth herbs. Let not him that eateth set at nought him that eateth not; and let not him that eateth not judge him that eateth: for God hath received him. Who art thou that judgest the servant of another? to his own lord he standeth or falleth. Yea, he shall be made to stand; for the Lord hath power to make him stand. One man esteemeth one day above another: another esteemeth every day alike. Let each man be fully assured in his own mind. He that regardeth the day, regardeth it unto the Lord: and he that eateth, eateth unto the Lord, for he giveth God thanks; and he that eateth not, unto the Lord he eateth not, and giveth God thanks. For none of us liveth to himself, and none dieth to himself. For whether we live, we live unto the Lord; or whether we die, we die unto the Lord: whether we live therefore, or die, we are the Lord's. For to this end Christ died, and lived again, that he might be Lord of both the dead and the living. But thou, why dost thou judge thy brother? or thou again, why dost thou set at nought thy brother? for we shall all stand before the judgement-seat of God. For it is written,

As I live, saith the Lord, to me every knee shall bow, And every tongue shall confess to God[15].

So then each one of us shall give account of himself to God.

Let us not therefore judge one another any more: but judge ye this rather, that no man put a stumblingblock in his brother's way, or an occasion of falling. I know, and am persuaded in the Lord Jesus, that nothing is unclean of itself: save that to him who accounteth anything to be unclean, to him it is unclean. For if because of meat thy brother is grieved, thou walkest no longer in love. Destroy not with thy meat him for whom Christ died. Let not then your good be evil spoken of: for the kingdom of God is not eating and drinking, but righteousness and peace and joy in the Holy Ghost. For he that herein serveth Christ is well-pleasing to God, and approved of men. So then let us follow after things which make for peace, and things whereby we may edify one another. Overthrow not for meat's sake the work of God. All things indeed are clean; howbeit it is evil for that man who eateth with offence. It is good not to eat flesh, nor to drink wine, nor to do anything whereby thy brother stumbleth. The faith which thou hast, have thou to thyself before God. Happy is he that judgeth not himself in that which he approveth. But he that doubteth is condemned if he eat, because he eateth not of faith; and whatsoever is not of faith is sin.

1. According to St. Paul a catholic church ought to mean a tolerant church, and a 'good catholic' a large-hearted Christian. If men of all races, with all sorts of traditional instincts and habits, were to live together in close social cohesion in the Christian community—and that was essential—this must involve much mutual forbearance, much self-restraint, and deliberate toleration of differences[16]. St. Paul plainly not merely uses, but loves, the language of toleration. 'One man eateth, another man eateth not,' 'One man esteemeth one day above another; another esteemeth every day alike. Let each man be fully assured in his own mind,' 'Receive ye him ... not with a

view to decisions of disputed questions.' Thoroughly in St. Paul's spirit is the familiar saying 'in necessary things unity: in those less than necessary liberty: in all things charity[17].'

In necessary things unity. To St. Paul this principle meant a clear limit to toleration. There is a common teaching which lies at the basis of the Church which must not be interfered with, which is strictly necessary. 'Though we, or an angel from heaven, should preach unto you any gospel other than that which we preached unto you, let him be anathema[18].' 'How say some among you that there is no resurrection of the dead? But if there is no resurrection of the dead, neither hath Christ been raised: and if Christ hath not been raised, then is our preaching vain, your faith also is vain[19].' Plainly there is an essential fundamental creed which must not be trifled with. The same is true about the moral law. In respect of that also the Christian body must exercise upon its members the severity of judgement[20], that 'he that hath done' the evil deed 'might be taken away from among them,' or excommunicated. Once more, we cannot conceive St. Paul making the necessity of visible unity a secondary consideration[21], nor the recognition of the authority of the apostolic ministry which is to be the centre of unity, nor the sacraments, which again are not only means of divine grace to the individual but instruments and bonds of unity. Nor again would St. Paul undervalue the spirit of obedience to the rules of the Church. He hates the spirit of heresy or separatism. 'We have no such custom,' he would say to the recalcitrant, 'neither the churches of God[22].' Once again, St. Paul is prepared to let everything turn on even a small and unessential point, if that point has become the symbol of a vital principle for good or evil. Thus, in itself, 'circumcision was nothing,' but when among the Galatians the practice of it came to mean a practical Judaizing— a practical abandonment of the fundamental Christian principle—then 'Behold, I Paul say unto you, that, if ye receive circumcision, Christ will profit you nothing[23].'

Here, then, are St. Paul's essentials, as to which he is intolerant—a fundamental tradition of faith and morals: the maintenance of the unity of the body by means of the apostolic stewardship, and through the 'one baptism,' and the 'one loaf': and the spirit of due subordination which is necessary to corporate life. But in a spirit very unlike what has at times become prevalent in the Church, he would clearly minimize the action of authority, and leave large room for the free movement of conscience in Christians. 'Let us therefore, as many as be perfect, be thus minded: and if in anything ye are otherwise minded, even this shall God reveal unto you: only, whereunto we have already attained, by that same rule let us walk[24].'

Surely it is not very difficult to apply this spirit of St. Paul to our own time, in view of those subordinate points which excite such deep animosities.

Men are by fundamental disposition, in great measure, ritualist or puritan, ecclesiastically or individually minded, disciplinarian or mystical. And the Church should lay on all a certain common law of doctrine and morals and worship, sufficient to keep them all together in one body. But, consistently with the coherence of the body, why should there not be both an ornate and a bare ritual of worship, both societies of strict observance and individual freedom, and a wide field of open questions in which we do not even expect 'decisions of doubts'? Instead of my own reflections on this subject I will ask my readers' attention to the following extracts from a suggestive book[25].

'At all times there are those to whom what we may call the minor symbolism of ritual is far from being as helpful as it is to others. There is the greatest diversity here. Modes of worship, which repel one man as bleak and bare, attract another by their very simplicity. The diversity is so natural and so obvious that it calls for neither apology nor explanation; yet it is easily strained into a cause of disruption.'

'St. Paul is speaking of strong brethren and of weak; of those who need earthly guides and of those who do not; of those who attach high value to rules and forms and helps; and of those for whom ordinances have but little significance; of mystics and disciplinarians.'

'Again, do we not still want a scientific theology? I mean a theology which should do what any scientific treatise does. It should lay down clearly and plainly the essential conditions of unity, and as regards the unessential should content itself with saying, "Here men differ; one thinks thus, another thus." ... Ask yourself, What is it that will carry me, being what I am, to heaven? What is it will carry my brother here, who is so unlike me, to heaven? What is it that will carry us both to heaven? There you will find the essential.'

St. Paul, we observe, lays great stress upon honesty of conscience. He wishes men, even in small matters, seriously to cultivate a conscience of what is right, as men should do who even in small things expect a divine judgement; and seriously also to cultivate the faculty of not interfering with their brother's conscience. ('Hast thou faith? Have it to thyself.' Do not parade your superior enlightenment.) He is greatly afraid of people leading others, or being led for mere agreement's sake, to do what their own conscience does not justify. And to do even a good thing because another does it whom we want to be like, without ourselves feeling sure it is good, or with a doubtful conscience[26], this, St. Paul says, is sin. This warning we really need to lay to heart in our age, when fashion is such a very strong force in religion. This individual follows that individual and 'supposes it must be all right, as every one seems to do it'; this congregation follows that congregation in adopting a popular practice, without its real basis and justification being considered. But fashion and the influence of members is a great danger in religion. 'Let every man be fully assured in his own mind.' 'Whatever is not of faith is sin[27].'

2. Plainly, when St. Paul wrote his epistles, there was no observance of a Sabbath obligatory upon Christians[28]. But was there none of Sunday? 'The first day of the week' was already 'the Lord's day,' so far as that Christians who could not meet to 'break the bread' every day, met on that day specially to commemorate the death of their risen Lord till He should come again[29]. It was already sufficiently distinctive for St. Paul to name it as the appropriate day for laying by alms for the poor[30]. But these special observances of it were not obligatory. Christians, when they could meet every day, might make their eucharist every day. No such observance of Sunday was yet enjoined as was incompatible with regarding all days of the week alike. Nothing less than this can satisfy St. Paul's words. In principle, as Bishop Lightfoot said[31], 'the kingdom of Christ has no sacred days or seasons, because every time alike is holy.'

Yet the bishop adds, 'appointed days are indispensable to her efficiency.' This was soon found to be the case. Probably before the end of the first century, the Didache mentions not only the observance of Sunday by the eucharistic service, but the observance also of the Wednesday and Friday fasts. Clement, about the same date, strongly emphasizes the principle of order in place and time, as still belonging to Christian worship. 'They, therefore, that make their offering at the appointed seasons are acceptable and blessed.' The Canons of Hippolytus show that by the end of the second century there must have been a great development of ecclesiastical regulations, so far restraining the individual liberty of the earliest days, and that, as far as we know, without protest or sense of alarm. Nor need St. Paul have been in opposition to such church rules. The spirit of regulation is strong in him[32]. On the other hand, there is no doubt that the Church has not generally, one might say has hardly ever, been conscious, as St. Paul was, of the danger of religious regulations as such. It is so much easier to keep certain rules than to acquire and maintain a certain mind and spirit and principle of action. In the history of the Church St. Paul, we feel, would very often have been saying, 'I am afraid of you: the rules are good in themselves, but there are dangers attaching to all rules of which you seem to be quite unconscious. There is a lower sort of religion of forms and observances, and you may fall back into it as easily as the Galatians.'

But after all, rules for living religiously, private or ecclesiastical, are, we all know, invaluable, and practically necessary. A man or a church that should attempt to dispense with them would come to disaster. It is very difficult to fathom the depth of the mischief that has come about in the corporate social life of the Church of England, through the neglect of the surely moderate amount of regulation which was provided for us by the Prayer Book in the way of festival and fast days and of daily service. To keep a few simple, intelligible, religious rules all together gives almost as much as a common creed the feeling of social coherence. Even the extremest Paulinist need have no fear so long as the ecclesiastical regulations do not reach the point of becoming a burden—so long as no one could be in danger of priding himself on 'acquiring merit' by their mere observance; and so long also as the principle is kept clearly in view that 'the rules were made for man and not man for the rules.' But I do not think there can be any reasonable doubt that St. Paul would repudiate the idea that any rules of worship and observance, other than those which are necessarily involved in the administration of the sacraments, can obtain by prescription a right to permanence. 'They may be changed according to the diversities of countries, times, and men's manners.' They were made for man; and the Church or the churches—with due regard to mutual fellowship—can modify or abolish them.

3. 'Overthrow not for meat's sake the work of God.' 'It is good not to eat flesh nor to drink wine, nor to do anything whereby thy brother stumbleth.' 'Wherefore, if meat maketh my brother to stumble, I will eat no flesh for evermore, that I make not my brother to stumble[33].' Here is the right principle of 'total abstinence' which does not deny the legitimate use of what it yet permanently abandons for love's sake. St. Paul would have Timothy use a little wine when it was for his health's sake, but when health was not in question, he would have all men ask, not how much liberty in this or that is lawful for them, but how they can avoid causing offence—how they can do most good. This principle admits of application in many directions. For instance, it may be very hard to determine why certain minor forms of gambling are wrong, or whether they are positively wrong. But St. Paul would have the other question asked—Can it be denied that the best way to avoid leading my brother into one of the most common dangers of our time, is to keep altogether free from a habit which in any case can do no good to body or mind?

4. Here, as in x. 7, St. Paul touches upon the descent into Hades, and indicates the purpose of it. 'For this end Christ died, that He might be Lord of the dead.' It might have been imagined that the dim realms of the dead were outside the jurisdiction of Christ—that the dead have no king—that the kingdom of redemption does not include them. To obviate such an idea, to show the universality of His realm, Christ went down among the dead.

5. In many places of the New Testament there is mention of the thanksgiving before food—the Christian's 'saying grace.' Whether he eat

flesh or vegetables he 'giveth God thanks[34].' And the word used is the word which, in its substantive form, is 'eucharist.' And indeed there is meaning in this. The thankful reception by the Christian of the ordinary bread of his daily life as coming from God, touched his common meals with something of the glory of divine communion; and the eucharist in its turn is the common blessing and breaking of the bread, raised by the Holy Spirit to a higher power and consecrated to become the vehicle of the bread of life[35].

[1] Possibly his mind passes by a natural reaction from the thought of sensual licentiousness (xiii. 13) to that of unenlightened asceticism.

[2] It is implied (xiv. 1; xv. 1 and 7) that the strong-minded brethren were in the ascendant. It is them chiefly to whom St. Paul addresses himself.

[3] Ecclus. xxxiii. 9.

[4] Mark vii. 19.

[5] Acts x. 28.

[6] The matter of 'eating with the Gentiles' was prominent, cf. ii. 12.

[7] 1 Cor. x. 25.

[8] Acts xv. 23.

[9] 1 Cor. viii, and x. 23-33.

[10] The exact point—abstaining from all flesh meat—is so different from what had presented itself at Corinth that there must be a particular reference to Roman circumstances, of which St. Paul was probably informed by Priscilla and Aquila.

[11] This seems to follow from Philo's statement that they did not make animal sacrifices: and from Josephus' description of their way of life as Pythagorean.

[12] Cf. 1 Cor. viii. 10.

[13] Gal. iv. 10; cf. Col. ii. 16, 17: 'Let no man therefore judge you in meat, or in drink, or in respect of a feast day or a new moon or a sabbath day: which are a shadow of the things to come; but the body is Christ's.'

[14] Or for decisions of doubts, marg. This, or something like this, is the right meaning; cf. Hebr. v. 14: 'for decision between good and evil.' 1 Cor. xii. 10: 'discernings of spirits,' i.e. decisions as to their true character.

[15] From Isa. xlv. 33.

[16] Cf. Ephes. pp. 271 f.

[17] See app. note H, p. 239.

[18] Gal. i. 8.

[19] 1 Cor. xv. 12, 13.

[20] 1 Cor. v. 6

[21] Cf. Ephes. p. 126.

[22] 1 Cor. xi. 16.

[23] Gal. v. 2.

[24] Phil. iii. 15, 16.

[25] Unity in Diversity, by Charles Bigg, D.D. (Longmans, 1899), pp. 84, 85, 95.

[26] 'Whatever is not of faith is sin—that is whatever is against conscience.' Aquinas, quoted in S. and H. in loc.

[27] Cf. xii. 6: 'Let us prophesy according to the proportion of our faith.'

[28] Col. ii. 16: 'Let no man judge you in respect of a sabbath day.'

[29] This is probably implied in Acts xx. 7.

[30] 1 Cor. xvi. 1.

[31] Philippians, on 'the Christian Ministry,' p. 181. The language in the immediate context I cannot make my own. But the statement quoted is surely true. And to this day I suppose, for those living in religious communities and similar institutions, there is very little practical difference between Sundays and week-days. This almost complete absence of distinction, however, must always come about, if it is to be legitimate, by raising the week-days to the spiritual level of the Sundays, and not by the opposite process.

[32] Especially in the Pastoral Epistles: but also in the epistles to the Thessalonians and Corinthians.

[33] 1 Cor. viii. 13.

[34] Cf. 1 Cor. x. 30: 'Why am I evil spoken of for that for which I give thanks.' 1 Tim. iv. 3, 4: 'Meats, which God created to be received with thanksgiving.... For every creature of God is good ... if it be received with thanksgiving: for it is sanctified through the word of God and prayer. Cf. Acts xxvii. 35: 'And when he had taken bread, he gave thanks to God in the presence of all: and he brake it, and began to eat.'

[35] Matt. xxvi. 26; cf. Luke xxiv. 30.

DIVISION V. § 7. CHAPTER XV. 1-13.

Unselfish forbearance and inclusiveness.

It was essential, as has been said, that men whose prejudices and instincts were different should live in the same church and eat at the same love feast. This would require a large-hearted and unselfish self-control. Formerly, as in Syria and Palestine, it was the Jews who occupied the position of vantage in the Christian communities, and were not disposed to tolerate the ways of the Gentiles. Now the tables are turned, and the Gentiles are in the majority. The danger is now that those whose instincts are Gentile should bear hardly upon the minority whose prejudices are more or less Jewish. Such St. Paul anticipates, or knows from Priscilla and Aquila, will be the danger among the Roman Christians. Formerly Judaic narrowness had been a formidable danger. It had developed a most perilous heresy, and St. Paul had dealt with it as a deadly poison. Now what remained of Jewish feeling was a weakness to be generously borne with. It affords St. Paul an opportunity of falling back on the general principle, that the measure of Christian strength and full-grown manhood is the readiness to bear the weaknesses of others.

To be told he must not use his normal liberty, must not eat his usual meal or drink his usual cup of wine, because it might scandalize some Christian with the ascetic prejudices of an Essene, or even induce him to do the same against his own conscience—to be told this was annoying to a man who held the 'strong' Christian conviction that all kinds of food were indifferently allowable. The weak scruple of his brother Christian had become an annoying burden of self-denial and self-restraint laid on himself. But this, St. Paul says, is how Christian strength—whether it be the moral strength of clear convictions, or any other sort of faculty[1]—must show itself, in readiness to suffer on account of other people's deficiencies, in not resenting the restraints they lay on us, in not expecting to do as we please, but being ready to accommodate ourselves to our neighbour's tastes where it is for his good. That is what our great example did. Plainly His whole human life was putting Himself under the restraints which our weaknesses and narrownesses and slownesses laid on Him. The righteous man in the psalm complains that he has to bear all the reproaches of God which impatient and rebellious Israelites might utter; and that is the picture of Christ bearing our infirmities. (The reproaches which fell on Him were for the very largeness of His love; 'because He received sinners,' and because He received them on the Sabbaths as well as on other days. They were reproaches of God, like Jonah's, because He was too forbearing, too generous.)

Then St. Paul pauses a moment to justify his use of the Psalms. These ancient scriptures did not fulfil their purpose in their own time, or for the old covenant. God intended them for Christians. Their teaching is what they need. The burdens of life are so many, its requirements upon their patience so constant, that they find it hard to maintain their hope. Yet what is the Old Testament so full of? Lessons of endurance and words of encouragement. The encouragement and endurance then, which they gain from the Old Testament, are to help them to maintain Christian hope. They must not lose heart. The end is a great one: it is the maintenance of a united spirit in the Church, such as Christ can approve, such as can express itself in a really unanimous adoration of Him whom Christ recognized as His God and Father. May the God who inspires endurance and encouragement, grant them not to fail in this great end!

Here is the central requirement, then, which a catholic church lays on them. It is to be unselfishly inclusive, to welcome into fellowship people who are not naturally to their taste. Our Lord did not scrutinize us men, but received us, of whatever sort we were, that God might be glorified in human brotherhood. He vindicated the truth of God by fulfilling the covenant of circumcision: first, to confirm the promises given to the fathers of Israel[2]; and, secondly, to enlarge the compass of Israel, so that the Gentiles too might share its blessings, out of God's pure mercy apart from any promises. And this also—the fellowship of Jew and Gentile—was matter of ancient prediction by psalmist and prophet. The Roman Christians must not therefore let themselves be discouraged because they have a difficult task to fulfil. And the apostle prays that God, the inspirer of hope, may fill them with such a rich sense of the blessings of believing in Him, that His Spirit, dwelling in them, may make hope to abound in their hearts.

Now we that are strong ought to bear the infirmities of the weak, and not to please ourselves. Let each one of us please his neighbour for that which is good, unto edifying. For Christ also pleased not himself; but, as it is written, The reproaches of them that reproached thee fell upon me. For whatsoever things were written aforetime were written for our learning, that through patience and through comfort of the scriptures we might have hope. Now the God of patience and of comfort grant you to be of the same mind one with another according to Christ Jesus: that with one accord ye may with one mouth glorify the God and Father of our Lord Jesus Christ. Wherefore receive ye one another, even as Christ also received you, to the glory of God. For I say that Christ hath been made a minister of the circumcision for the truth of God, that he might confirm the promises given unto the fathers, and that the Gentiles might glorify God for his mercy; as it is written,

Therefore will I give praise unto thee among the Gentiles,
And sing unto thy name.

And again he saith,

Rejoice, ye Gentiles, with his people.

And again,

Praise the Lord, all ye Gentiles;
And let all the peoples praise him.

And again, Isaiah saith,

There shall be the root of Jesse,
And he that ariseth to rule over the Gentiles;
On him shall the Gentiles hope.

Now the God of hope fill you with all joy and peace in believing, that ye may abound in hope, in the power of the Holy Ghost.

1. The connexion of thought in this passage is undoubtedly somewhat obscure. But we know to-day, as well as ever, how difficult it is to bear with what is disagreeable to us in others, with what seem to us their deficiencies, without breaking real Christian brotherhood and co-operation. And we know also that where we are possessed by an enthusiasm for brotherhood such as inspired the early Christians, the divisions which small differences tend to produce are peculiarly discouraging, because they suggest that real brotherhood is impossible where men are so differently constituted. We ought not, therefore, to be at a loss to see why St. Paul should pass so easily from speaking of divisions among Christians to speak of the grounds of patience and encouragement and hope. The Christian hope is—in substantial part—the hope of a really catholic church—a real brotherhood among people of different races, classes, tastes, and habits; and it is this great hope which, even in St. Paul's day, was continually suffering discouragement and continually needed reinforcing. And the reinforcement must be 'supernatural.' It is the divine love of the Spirit possessing us which alone can give it vigour. When we are full of the divine consolation, then it is that we are least inclined to be critical, and most disposed 'to receive one another, as Christ also received us, to the glory of God.' For this is the thought we are to have constantly in view, when we find people 'aggravating'—Christ received us, and made the best of those whom 'God gave him,' in spite of the infinite annoyances which we men, even the apostles, caused Him; He dealt with us with infinite patience; He made us welcome; He 'received us.'

In fact, the reason why the connexion of thought in this passage seems obscure to us, is probably in part that we have ceased to think of the real fellowship of the naturally unlike—fellowship in all that makes up human life—as a necessary part of the Christian religion. But to St. Paul there was no Christianity without the reality of catholic brotherhood.

2. St. Paul here, as in writing to the Corinthians[3], shows himself specially anxious that Gentile Christians should not think they could make light of the Old Testament, or imagine that 'Christ was the end of the law' in any such sense as would make the books of the old covenant superfluous under the new. Their value, he insists, remains permanent. When he is writing to the Corinthians, he finds it in the moral warnings—the warnings of divine judgement upon the chosen people—of which the history is full. In this epistle he is thinking chiefly of the lessons of 'endurance' and divine 'encouragements,' which histories and prophets provide. In his epistle to Timothy[4] he thinks of the books as instruments by the use of which the minister or representative of God may become fully educated and equipped for all the purposes of moral supervision and discipline. They can thus educate and equip him, St. Paul teaches, because they were originally written under the influence of a divine inspiration; but it is only when faith has finally attained its true object in Jesus Christ that their real meaning becomes apparent. And this last principle is implied in almost all his use of the Old Testament. It is a comfort to perceive that none of the elements of permanent value, which St. Paul discerns in the Old Testament, are the least likely to be affected by reasonable criticism of its documents. Its history, critically read, does not become less truly pregnant with moral warnings or lessons of endurance. The encouragements of the prophets are in no respect reduced in force when they are brought into right relation to their own times. The whole library of books is, at least, as capable of educating and equipping the minister of Christ as ever. Their inspiration is still obvious, when it is interpreted candidly in view of all the facts. And still they can only be rightly regarded when they are looked upon as various elements in a progress which has Christ for its goal. In his use of particular passages in the Old Testament St. Paul here shows himself as free as ever, but with the same fundamental adherence to the true tendency of the Old Testament as a whole. In quoting Ps. lxix. 9 (ver. 3) he is seeing in the afflicted righteous man a type of Christ. This psalm is constantly cited in the New Testament with the same reference[5]. It has been supposed[6] that St. Paul here adopts a cry addressed to God by the righteous sufferer in the psalm, and represents it as addressed by Christ to his brother man. 'The reproaches aimed at thee, my despised brother, have fallen upon me.' But, as I have tried to show in the analysis above, this supposition is not needed. Christ is represented appealing to God for succour, because He utterly refuses to take the line of self-pleasing; but bears all that men's

impatience of God lays upon Him—all their 'wild and weak complaining.' And it is suggestive to remember, with Origen, that it was Christ's 'receiving of sinners and eating with them,' receiving them on the Sabbath as well as other days, that chiefly brought on Him the reproaches of men. This was probably in St. Paul's mind. In Ps. xviii. 49 (quoted ver. 9) the victorious king declares that he will praise God for his victory 'among the nations.' St. Paul applies this to Christ, whose victory among the nations means their redemption—their becoming His people. In Deut. xxxii. 43 (ver. 10) 'the nations are invited to congratulate Israel on possessing a God like Jehovah, who will effectually take up His people's cause. Such an invitation addressed to the nations (cf. Isa. xlii. 10-12; Ps. xlvii. 2, lxvii. 1-7, &c.) involves implicitly the prophetic truth that God's dealings with Israel have indirectly an interest and importance for the world at large[7].' This is still more plainly implied in Ps. cxvii. 1 (ver. 11).

Isa. xi. 10 (ver. 12) is quoted from the Greek Bible, which is paraphrastic; but the Hebrew also asserts that the messianic king of David's line is to be a 'signal to the nations,' and that they are to 'resort to him' as to an oracle or place of refuge[8].

[1] We are all 'strong' in some respect, Origen remarks, so that 'ye that are strong bear the infirmities of the weak' comes to be as broad a precept as 'bear ye one another's burdens.'

[2] Cf. Gal. iv. 4, 5: 'Christ, born of a woman, born under the law, that he might redeem them which were under the law, that we (Jews and Gentiles) might receive the adoption of sons.'

[3] 1 Cor. x. ii: 'These things happened unto them (the Jews in the Wilderness) by way of example; and they were written for our admonition, upon whom the ends of the ages are come.'

[4] 2 Tim. iii. 15-17. 'Sacred writings which are able to make thee wise unto salvation through faith which is in Christ Jesus. Every scripture inspired by God is also profitable for teaching, for reproof, for correction, for instruction which is in righteousness: that the man of God may be complete, furnished completely unto every good work.'

[5] Cf. above, xi. 9; in the Gospels, Matt. xxvii. 34; John ii. 17; xix. 28; also Acts i. 20.

[6] See S. and H. in loc.

[7] Driver, in loc.

[8] Cheyne, in loc.

DIVISION VI. CHAPTERS XV. 14-XVI. 27.

Conclusion.

The long letter is almost ended. St. Paul has developed the meaning of the revelation of the divine righteousness. He has vindicated the ways of God to the Jews. He has drawn out sufficiently the moral conclusions from God's mercy to mankind. Now he has only to secure again his good terms with the Roman Christians—which he does with the same tact and the same anxiety as at the beginning[1],—to explain his movements, to send his greetings to individuals, and to bid farewell.

[1] Vol. i. p. 53.

DIVISION VI. § 1. CHAPTER XV. 14-33.

His excuse for writing and his hope of coming.

St. Paul is very anxious not to be understood as if, while giving the Christians at Rome these exhortations which we have just been reading, he stood in any doubt himself of their goodness of heart and full grasp of Christian principles, or of their fitness to admonish one another. He has only been bold to put them in mind of what they already knew, because of the priestly commission on behalf of his Lord towards all the Gentiles, which the divine grace has bestowed upon him as apostle of the Gentiles. The gospel entrusted to him requires him as a priest to prepare and offer sacrifice; and the sacrifice which he is to prepare, which the consecration of the indwelling Spirit alone can make acceptable, is that of the whole Gentile world. The extent to which this great charge laid upon him has been fulfilled, gives him good reason for boasting as he stands before God—not in himself, but in Christ Jesus. His work has been a pioneer's work. He has made it his ambition purely to lay foundations. Taking words of Isaiah[1] for his motto, he had resolved to go nowhere where any other had been before him to make Christ known. But in that free and open area of a yet unevangelized world, Christ had worked through him to bring the Gentiles to His obedience, and had accompanied his preaching with evidences of miraculous power and with the strong manifestations of the Spirit. So that in the result the work of proclaiming the gospel had been accomplished, starting from Jerusalem, in an extending circuit[2] or irregular progress, as far as Illyria.

This world-wide mission would give St. Paul his title to visit Rome[3]. But its very greatness has hitherto hindered him. Now however he is hoping to satisfy the desire that has so long possessed him, and to pay them a visit of some length on his way to Spain. That is to say, he hopes to come to them when the task is over which is immediately occupying him. The good will of the churches in Macedonia and Achaia has shown itself in a collection of money for the poor Christians at Jerusalem. This is really the payment of a debt to those to whom they owe their fellowship in Christ's salvation. When then St. Paul has handed over this collection, and secured to its recipients this fruit of his mission, he hopes to pass to Spain by way of Rome; and again, as in his introduction[4], he expresses his confidence that at Rome, as elsewhere, the fullness of the rich gifts of Christ will accompany his coming.

Meanwhile he makes his urgent request, by their allegiance to Christ and their fellowship in the spirit of love, that they will join with him in wrestling with God in prayer for the success of his present undertaking—that he may escape the danger to which he is exposed from the hostility of the unbelieving Jews, and that the gift, as ministered by him, may not prove unacceptable to the Jerusalem church; so that he may get happily to Rome and find repose there with them. And he prays for the blessing of the God of peace upon all of them.

And I myself also am persuaded of you, my brethren, that ye yourselves are full of goodness, filled with all knowledge, able also to admonish one another. But I write the more boldly unto you in some measure, as putting you again in remembrance, because of the grace that was given me of God, that I should be a minister of Christ Jesus unto the Gentiles, ministering[5] the gospel of God, that the offering up of the Gentiles might be made acceptable, being sanctified by the Holy Ghost. I have therefore my glorying in Christ Jesus in things pertaining to God. For I will not dare to speak of any things save those which Christ wrought through me, for the obedience of the Gentiles, by word and deed, in the power of signs and wonders, in the power of the Holy Ghost; so that from Jerusalem, and round about even unto Illyricum, I have fully preached the gospel of Christ; yea, making it my aim so to preach the gospel, not where Christ was already named, that I might not build upon another man's foundation; but, as it is written,

They shall see, to whom no tidings of him came,
And they who have not heard shall understand.

Wherefore also I was hindered these many times from coming to you: but now, having no more any place in these regions, and having these many years a longing to come unto you, whensoever I go unto Spain (for I hope to see you in my journey, and to be brought on my way thitherward by you, if first in some measure I shall have been satisfied with your company)— but now, I say, I go unto Jerusalem, ministering unto the saints. For it hath been the good pleasure of Macedonia and Achaia to make a certain contribution for the poor among the saints that are at Jerusalem. Yea, it hath been their good pleasure; and their debtors they are. For if the Gentiles have been made partakers of their spiritual things, they owe it to them also to minister unto them in carnal things. When therefore I have accomplished this, and have sealed to them this fruit, I will go on by you unto Spain. And I know that, when I come unto you, I shall come in the fulness of the blessing of Christ.

Now I beseech you, brethren, by our Lord Jesus Christ, and by the love of the Spirit, that ye strive together with me in your prayers to God for me; that I may be delivered from them that are disobedient in Judaea, and that my ministration which I have for Jerusalem may be acceptable to the saints;

that I may come unto you in joy through the will of God, and together with you find rest. Now the God of peace be with you all. Amen.

1. St. Paul has a habit of representing those he writes to in the best light[6]. But the words 'full of goodness,' 'filled with all knowledge,' 'able to admonish,' are no idle compliments. It is not too much to suggest that St. Paul, as he sees the high part which the church of the capital must play in the world, perceives also, in what he hears of the Roman Christians, evidences of the spirit which will enable them to fulfil it. And history verifies the apostle's anticipation. The letter of the Roman church to the Corinthians, which passes under Clement's name, and was written some forty years after this letter of St. Paul's, is the very embodiment of the spirit of goodness, knowledge, and power to admonish. The princely generosity of the Roman church in all directions was proverbial in the second century[7]. If it did not become as distinguished as Alexandria in theological science, it did become a chief centre of theological orthodoxy and government. And the repeated evidences we gain that rigorists, from Hippolytus to Novatian, were so dissatisfied with the policy of the Roman bishops as to separate themselves from their communion, give us good reason to believe that the internal policy of this church was, within just limits, liberal and tolerant.

2. St. Paul here describes his apostolic commission in priestly language. 'The sacrificial terminology is far more marked in the original than it can be in a translation[8].' The word for 'minister of Christ Jesus' is a technical word for priest in the Greek Old Testament[9]. The word translated 'ministering' means 'offering sacrifice.' (That which St. Paul describes himself as offering in sacrifice is not the gospel, as our translation might imply: the gospel assigns the sphere of the sacrifice[10], but the sacrifice he has to offer is that of the Gentile world, in Christ, consecrated to be a fit sacrifice by the Spirit.) The phrase also, 'in things pertaining to God' (cf. Hebr. ii. 17), is appropriate to the priest as he stands before God. 'But this is all symbolical language,' it is said. That depends on what we take as the standard of reality in the sacrificing priesthood. If Christ is the standard of priesthood, and His method of making sacrifice the standard method, then St. Paul's account of his priestliness is not appreciably metaphorical, except so far as metaphor belongs to all earthly expressions of heavenly realities; it is rather true to say that the Jewish or heathen priest, with his material victims, was but the dim shadow of a true priest.

The point is that the true Christian idea of sacrifice makes the substance of it to be always persons returning to God the life He gave them. If we must offer sacrifices of money and fruits of the earth, that is because we cannot offer ourselves without our bodies[11], or our bodies without the material supplies on which they depend. 'All things come of God, and of His own do we give Him.' And all our labour and prayer for others must be an offering of them, or a preparation to offer them[12], to God; which again is only our assisting them to offer themselves. And all this offering in sacrifice of ourselves and others is rendered possible by the one effectual sacrifice, through which alone we and all men have access to the Father. It takes place 'in Christ Jesus,' who, 'through eternal Spirit offered himself without spot to God.' There, at the head of all, is the sacrifice of the person, and that person the Son of Man, who can take up into His very life and sacrifice even all mankind. Throughout it is a sacrifice of persons, or of things only as appertaining to persons. This is the fundamental Christian idea, and this at the bottom necessarily forbids us to separate the thing offered from the person offering, the victim from the priest. The priest is the victim, for what he offers is himself.

It is this idea of sacrifice which is realized in the eucharist. The eucharist is the central sacrifice of the Christian body. It is to start with a presentation of material things, bread and wine of the fruits of the earth, with alms and other offerings it may be: and these oblations are accompanied with prayers and symbolic rites. But all is done that both by word and act the One Sacrifice may be commemorated and pleaded. The outward rite but finds its meaning and justification in that—the sacrifice of the Person. Again we can only take part in it with any spiritual reality by becoming ourselves sharers of His sacrifice—ourselves the sacrifice we offer. 'And here,' we cry, 'we offer and present unto Thee ourselves.' We men, St. Augustine does not scruple to say, are the body of Christ, which is offered in that sacrifice[13]. And a quite new light is shed on intercessory prayer, in the eucharist and in the rest of life, when we view it as St. Paul would have us view it, as a presenting in sacrifice before God those for whom we pray, according to the true idea of them which the sanctification of the Spirit would make possible and actual. And a quite new light is shed upon all work for others, when we regard it as the preparing of such a sacrifice for the Holy Spirit to consecrate.

From a different point of view St. Paul's conception of his mission as the priest of the Gentile world, might well suggest reflections to the Church of England. If a Christian nation in the providence of God is to overrun the world and possess the nations not yet Christian, it goes with a mission entrusted to it by God. Its mission may be expressed, according to St. Paul's idea, as that of evangelizing the world, but also as that of preparing the heathen nations to be offered to God. It is the return of all humanity to Himself that God desires, and we are to be the ministers of this perfected offering. It strikes us with profound humiliation to realize how 'far fetched' St. Paul's idea would appear to-day to the mass of our nation, which, more than any other, is called by circumstances to an apostolate of the world.

3. St. Paul speaks, here and in many places elsewhere, of his grounds for 'glorying,' or rather 'boasting[14],' in what Christ has wrought through him, and of his 'being ambitious' to preach only where no one had been before him[15]. And in reading such passages the question sometimes arises in Christian minds—was there, after all, a strain of egotism unsubdued in St. Paul's character? Now no doubt, unlike other apostles whose writings remain in the New Testament, St. Paul had that sort of passionately personal and individual nature which easily passes into spiritual egotism. This at least is discernible in his epistles. It is also true that the necessity which lay so long upon him of vindicating his own apostolic authority, makes it necessary for him at times to talk about himself and his experiences and his personal methods in a way that to some minds suggests egotism; and there is no obligation upon us to maintain that St. Paul was perfect. But we only understand these passages aright when we remember that there runs through them all a conscious irony. The basis of St. Paul's whole theology was the denial of any possible ground for a man to boast in himself. 'Where is boasting? it is excluded.' 'He that boasteth, let him boast in the Lord.' It is Christ who 'leads St. Paul in' His 'triumph.' What he boasts of is not his own, but Christ's. Of course, this sort of language very easily admits of self-deception. St. Paul shows himself conscious of its danger[16]. But there can be no question of the vehement sincerity of St. Paul in repudiating any homage to himself which seemed to put him in the place of Christ, or to substitute the teacher for his message[17]. And where his personal gifts of intellect might most easily have shone, he had determined to abjure all 'the wisdom of men' in the method of his preaching[18]. It is remarkable again that as soon as ever the real peril from Judaism was over in the Church, St. Paul drops his anti-Judaistic polemic, and all that brings the personal element into prominence. He is absolutely free from the charge of pursuing his advantage so as to magnify a personal victory. The more thoroughly we grow to know St. Paul, the more, I think, we feel that his profession is true that he will 'boast' only 'in the cross of our Lord Jesus Christ'; and that truly the world, with all its personal ambitions, had been for him nailed to the cross and killed[19].

But what exactly was it that St. Paul had to 'boast' that Christ had wrought through him?

He had, he says, accomplished the preaching of the gospel in an irregular circuit from Jerusalem to Illyria. After he had made a beginning of Christian preaching at Damascus, he had, in fact, shared the apostolic preaching at Jerusalem (Acts ix. 29), but his own special work began at Tarsus, or rather at Antioch. After that he had 'fulfilled the proclamation of the gospel,' so far, that is to say, as it belonged to the apostolic office, by founding churches in a gradually enlarging circuit, especially in the chief centres, as the narrative of the Acts shows us, till travelling by the Egnatian way he would have come within sight of the Illyrian mountains at Thessalonica[20]. He may even have entered Illyria when the Acts vaguely describes him as going to Macedonia and then 'passing through those parts[21]'; but the expression in this epistle does not require this. It is sufficient that the border of Illyria, through which the Egnatian way led to Rome, had been so far his nearest point to the capital.

St. Paul certainly implies that Rome was included in his province of work, and that he owed them a yet unpaid debt[22]. This must surely mean, according to St. Paul's principle, that no other of the greater apostles had yet evangelized them or founded the church there[23]. Rome was no other man's foundation. But none the less, the elements of a church had collected there. The gospel was being preached there by 'apostles' from among his own circle. And St. Paul, for this reason, does not contemplate any permanent stay with the Romans, but regards Rome only as a place where he can rest and refresh himself, as well as supply deficiencies in the spiritual equipment of the church there, before he passes further west to the untouched region of Spain. St. Paul, we see plainly enough, had no power to foresee the future. But after the long residence at Rome during his first captivity, which he did not the least anticipate, did he, we ask, actually get to Spain? There is certainly no good reason to say he did not, for his movements are, in the main, unknown to us in the last period of his life; and on the other hand in Clement's letter to the Corinthians, written within the first century, he is said to have passed before his martyrdom to 'the limits of the west'—the extreme west—which is certainly most naturally interpreted of Spain[24].

4. St. Paul speaks of having wrought 'signs and wonders.' The two words are habitually combined in the New Testament. The word 'wonders' describes the miraculous and astonishing character of the events, while 'signs' indicates that moral witness and significance which distinguishes Christian miracles from vulgar portents. We read of St. Paul working miracles in the Acts. What he says here, and elsewhere[25], implies that they were frequently worked, and especially at Corinth, where no such events are recorded in the history. What it is important for us to recognize is, that St. Paul so plainly and repeatedly appeals, in the face of those who could bear witness, to the fact that he himself had power given to him to work miracles, as if it were indisputable.

5. St. Paul tells us that he had it specially laid upon him by the apostles of the circumcision that he was to 'remember the poor,' i.e. the poor Christians at Jerusalem; where poverty was specially rife, because, as we should gather, the wealthier Jews had held aloof from Christianity[26]. And this, he adds, was the very thing he himself was zealous to do[27]. How

much it was in his mind, both the Acts and his own epistles bear witness. We hear much in the epistles to the Corinthians[28] of the collection made in the churches of Macedonia and Achaia. Not only was this expression of Gentile good will intended to conciliate the half-alienated and suspicious Jewish Christians of Jerusalem, but the acceptance of the gift at St. Paul's hands, as the fruit of his own labour, was to diminish their suspicion of himself. St. Paul was at pains to prevent any suspicion attaching to his administration of this bounty, and at every point we perceive how much trouble he took about the matter. But, hopeful and zealous as he was about this work of charity, he did not underrate its dangers. His urgent request for the Roman Christians' prayers in this passage, and his readiness to meet his death, if need be, at Jerusalem, as expressed in the narrative of the Acts, show us that he knew the danger he was incurring from the fierce hostility of the Jerusalem Jews.

6. This passage about the collection[29], coupled with the allusion to Cenchreae, the port of Corinth, at the beginning of the next chapter, and the allusion to the Corinthian Gaius as St. Paul's host[30], enable us to fix the occasion of the writing of this epistle exactly at the moment recorded in Acts xx. 3—the end of his three months' residence in Greece. We also gather from the Acts[31], as well as from this epistle, that it was his intention at that period, when he had paid his visit to Jerusalem, to go to Rome. Once more we know from the Acts[32] that Sosipater and Timothy were with him at this point, and they join in the greetings of the epistle[33]. So that all the indications taken together fix with wonderful accuracy the exact point when the epistle was written[34].

7. We do well to note the word used by St. Paul in asking the Roman Christians' prayers. He begs them to 'strive together' with him in their prayers. This word is a derivative of that which describes our Lord's 'agony' in prayer; and Origen's comment upon it is this: 'Hardly any one can pray without some idle and alien thought coming into his mind, and leading off and interrupting the intended direction of his mind to God.... And, therefore, prayer is a great striving (agon, wrestling), so that the fixed direction of the soul towards God may be maintained, in spite of the enemies which interfere and seek to scatter the sense of prayer; so that one who prays may justly say, with St. Paul, "I have fought a good fight; I have finished my course."'

[1] lii. 15, according to the Greek.

[2] 'Round about,' literally 'in a circle,' as opposed to a straight course; cf. Mark vi. 6, 'round about the villages.'

[3] Cf. i. 13-16.

[4] i. 11.

[5] 'Ministering in sacrifice' marg.

[6] Cf. the opening of 1 Cor., a letter which contains on the whole so much blame.

[7] Euseb. H. E. iv. 23.

[8] Sanday, Conception of Priesthood (Longmans), p. 89.

[9] Like 'agape' (see above, p. 131, n. 2) so this word 'liturgus' appears to have been adopted in its priestly sense by the Greek translators of the Bible from the current Greek of Alexandria, cf. Deissmann, Bibelstudien, pp. 137 f.

[10] Cf. S. and H. in loc. 'Making sacrifice as a priest under the Gospel.'

[11] Cf. xii. x.

[12] Col. i. 28: 'Teaching every man ... that we may present every man,' i.e. present him in sacrifice.

[13] For his repeated statements see app. note I. p. 240.

[14] Cf. 1 Cor. ix. 15; xv. 31; 2 Cor. i. 14; vii. 4, 14; viii. 24; ix. 3; x. 8, 13; xi. 10, 16-xii. 9; Phil. ii. 16; 1 Thess. ii. 19. These passages are worth examining in connexion.

[15] Cf. 2 Cor. x. 15, 16.

[16] See 2 Cor. xi. 17; xii. 1.

[17] 1 Cor. i. 13 ff.

[18] 1 Cor. ii. 1-5.

[19] Gal. vi. 14.

[20] See S. and H. in loc.

[21] Acts xx. 2.

[22] i. 14, 15.

[23] Not Peter therefore, though he was doubtless afterwards at Rome.

[24] Ad Cor. 5, see Lightfoot in loc.

[25] 2 Cor. xii. 13.

[26] Cf. Jas. ii. 5, 6.

[27] Gal. ii. 10.

[28] 1 Cor. xvi. 1-4; 2 Cor. viii, ix.

[29] Cf. Acts xxiv. 17.

[30] Rom. xvi. 23. Cf. 1 Cor. i. 14, which shows us a Gaius at Corinth. Cf. the allusion to Erastus in the same verse, coupled with 2 Tim. iv. 20.

[31] Acts xix. 21.

[32] Acts xx. 4.

[33] Rom. xvi. 21.

[34] See further, on the purpose of the epistle, vol. i. pp. 4 ff.

DIVISION VI. § 2. CHAPTER XVI. 1-2.

A commendation.

One strong link among Christians of different towns, constraining them to remember that their brotherhood did not depend on physical nearness or personal acquaintance, lay in the 'letters of commendation' from one local church to another, which the Christian traveller carried with him. And here we have an example of such a letter given by St. Paul to the Corinthian deaconess, Phoebe, who was probably the bearer of his letter to the Roman Christians.

I commend unto you Phoebe our sister, who is a servant[1] of the church that is at Cenchreae: that ye receive her in the Lord, worthily of the saints, and that ye assist her in whatsoever matter she may have need of you: for she herself also hath been a succourer of many, and of mine own self.

The necessity of instructing women inquirers or catechumens, visiting them at their homes, preparing them for baptism, attending to their unclothing and reclothing at the font, and looking after them afterwards, forced upon the Church the institution of an order of deaconesses, side by side with the deacons and for similar purposes. Pliny found these female officers among the Christians in Bithynia in the beginning of the second century, and there is no reason why already at this date the female order should not have existed[2]. 'Here we learn,' says Origen on this passage, 'that female ministers are recognized in the Church.'

Phoebe is also called a succourer or 'patroness' of Christians, including St. Paul, which suggests a woman of wealth and influence. If so, we have here an example of wealth, not asserting itself but devoting itself to service, according to our Lord's teaching: 'He that is greatest among you shall be your servant (deacon)'; 'I am in the midst of you as he that serveth (the deacon)[3].' Such an one is to be received in a manner 'worthy of the saints,' the consecrated family of God, and to be allowed to lack nothing which the Roman Christians can supply her with.

[1] Or deaconess, as margin.

[2] See on this subject Deaconess Cecilia Robinson, The Ministry of Deaconesses (Methuen, 1898), and Bernard, Pastoral Epistles, p. 59. With Lightfoot, he interprets 1 Tim. iii. 11 of deaconesses rather than of the wives of the deacons.

[3] Matt, xxiii. 11; Luke xxii. 37.

DIVISION VI. § 3. CHAPTER XVI. 3-16.

Personal greetings.

Then St. Paul, according to his custom, winds up his epistle with personal greetings. In this case they are sent to the individual Christians, among those who from various parts of the empire had collected at Rome, whose names his memory—so retentive of personal relationships—enabled him to recall.

Salute Prisca and Aquila my fellow-workers in Christ Jesus, who for my life laid down their own necks; unto whom not only I give thanks, but also all the churches of the Gentiles: and salute the church that is in their house. Salute Epaenetus my beloved, who is the firstfruits of Asia unto Christ. Salute Mary, who bestowed much labour on you. Salute Andronicus and Junias[1], my kinsmen, and my fellow-prisoners, who are of note among the apostles, who also have been in Christ before me. Salute Ampliatus my beloved in the Lord. Salute Urbanus our fellow-worker in Christ, and Stachys my beloved. Salute Apelles the approved in Christ. Salute them which are of the household of Aristobulus. Salute Herodion my kinsman. Salute them of the household of Narcissus, which are in the Lord. Salute Tryphaena and Tryphosa, who labour in the Lord. Salute Persis the beloved, which laboured much in the Lord. Salute Rufus the chosen in the Lord, and his mother and mine. Salute Asyncritus, Phlegon, Hermes, Patrobas, Hermas, and the brethren that are with them. Salute Philologus and Julia, Nereus and his sister, and Olympas, and all the saints that are with them. Salute one another with a holy kiss. All the churches of Christ salute you.

1. Aquila, a Pontic Jew, had resided in Rome, doubtless in pursuit of his business as a tent-maker; but the edict of Claudius had compelled him to quit the capital in common with his brethren, and he had taken refuge at Corinth with his wife Prisca (as St. Paul calls her), or Priscilla (according to St. Luke[2]); and there, shortly after their arrival, St. Paul had found them, made their acquaintance, and combined with them in a common trade. To this was possibly due their conversion to Christianity. When St. Paul left Corinth, they accompanied him to Ephesus, and remained there when he left for Jerusalem; their influential position in the Christian community being indicated to us by their dealings with so important a teacher as Apollos. When St. Paul had returned to Ephesus, and was writing his First Epistle to the Corinthians, their house was the centre for a Christian congregation[3]. It was possibly during the Ephesian disturbances that they risked their lives, or 'laid down their own necks' for St. Paul. Whether on

account of this peril incurred, or for whatever reason, they returned, as they were now free to do, to Rome. The Epistle to the Romans follows the First Epistle to the Corinthians by not more than a year, and it finds Prisca and Aquila established at Rome, with a church meeting at their house. Probably they had been St. Paul's informants as to affairs among the Roman Christians. A good many years afterwards, when St. Paul was writing his Second Epistle to Timothy[4], we hear of them again at Ephesus. So much travelling as we find in their life was not unusual in the Roman empire, and perhaps least of all among the Jews.

The fact that Priscilla is generally mentioned before her husband, both by St. Paul and St. Luke[5], as if she were more important, combined with (1) a tradition which connects her with the titulus (or parish-church) Priscae at Rome, (2) evidence connecting the Coemeterium Priscillae with the Acilian gens,—has led some scholars to believe that Priscilla was a noble Roman lady married to a Jewish husband. But the evidence is not cogent, and it is more likely that both she and her husband owed their Roman names to being freedmen[6]. It was probably her prominence among the Christians which led to her name preceding that of her husband. We need only think of Phoebe and Priscilla to understand how influential women were in the earliest Christian churches.

'The church (which met) at their house' is a significant phrase[7]. The wealthier Christians, or those whose houses were commodious, turned them into churches, where the neighbouring Christians met for worship, love feast and eucharist. Several of the oldest churches in Rome grew in this manner out of private houses.

2. St. Paul's brief characterizations of individuals are full of personal memory and tenderness—'my beloved, who is the firstfruits of Asia unto Christ[8],' 'who bestowed much labour on you,' 'my kinsmen (i.e. Jews) and fellow prisoners (on some occasion which we cannot fix, but which St. Paul remembers), who also were in Christ before me,' 'our fellow worker,' 'the man approved in Christ,' who has been tried and found not wanting, 'his mother and mine.' St. Paul, notwithstanding his wide ecclesiastical plans and theological labours, as he thought no pains too much to bestow on the details of his scheme for collecting Gentile money for the needs of poor Jews, so also never lets great designs obscure the memory of persons and their intricate relations to himself.

3. Andronicus and Junias (or junianus) are 'of note among the apostles.' There are other indications that the term 'apostle' was not confined to the twelve. Not St. Paul only, but Barnabas also, and the Lord's brother, were included in it. Later, in the Didache, we find it used in a wide but somewhat dim sense, for the chief teachers of the Church who were not settled in

particular churches[9]. Nevertheless, this passage describing two men of unknown names as 'conspicuous among the apostles' is surprising. Probably the real requirement for sharing the title of apostle was to have received commission from the Lord (as 'other seventy' did besides the Twelve), and to have seen Him after His resurrection. These two—'early disciples' as St. Paul tells us—may have fulfilled these requirements. They were Jews like himself, who with him had laboured and suffered. They would be centres of authority among the Christians at Rome[10]: and possibly to the laying on of their hands other brethren at Rome who 'ruled' or 'taught' or 'ministered' owed their qualifying gift.

Chrysostom takes the second name to be a woman's—Junia; and expresses his astonishment at finding a woman thought worthy of the title of an apostle.

4. 'Them that are of the household of Aristobulus.' This Aristobulus was very probably the grandson of Herod the Great, who lived and died at Rome in a private station, and whose 'household' would naturally include many Jews and orientals. The following name of a Jew suggests connexion with the Herods.

5. 'Rufus' may very likely be the son of Simon of Cyrene, whom St. Mark, writing probably at Rome, refers to as well known[11].

6. 'A holy kiss.' 'It was from this and similar words,' says Origen, 'that it has been handed down as a custom in the Church that after the prayer the brethren should welcome one another with a kiss.' He goes on to urge that this ritual kiss should be neither unchaste nor without real feeling.

7. 'All the churches of Christ salute you.' This unique phrase is probably used, as Dr. Hort suggests, to express how 'the church of Rome was an object of love and respect to Jewish and Gentile churches alike.'

[1] Or Junia (a woman's name), as margin.

[2] See the readings of Rom. xvi. 3; 1 Cor. xvi. 19; 2 Tim. iv. 19 (in R. V. which is probably right); and of Acts xviii. 2, 18, 26.

[3] 1 Cor. xvi. 19.

[4] 2 Tim. iv. 19.

[5] Twice out of three mentions in each case.

[6] Perhaps both freedmen of the same member of the Acilian gens. For Priscus or Prisca (or Priscilla) was a favourite cognomen in the gens, and the nomen itself was commonly written Aquilius. This nomen a male slave, when freed, would have borne (besides his own name and his master's praenomen); and a female could have borne the cognomen Prisca or

Priscilla. '[Greek] Akúlios could be corrupted into {Greek] Akúlas, the Greek form of a different name Aquila.

[7] Cf. Acts xii. 12; Col. iv. 15; Philem. 2. See S. and H. in loc.

[8] Cf. 1 Cor. xvi. 15.

[9] The term 'apostle' is also used in 2 Cor. viii. 23, Phil. ii. 25, apparently in the sense of messenger.

[10] Others, including Liddon, would translate 'highly esteemed among, i.e. by, the apostles' but this is not probable.

[11] Mark xv. 21.

DIVISION VI. § 4. CHAPTER XVI. 17-20.

Final warning.

Something occurred before the letter to the Romans was concluded and dispatched to make St. Paul insert a final warning against false teachers, who were causing divisions and perverting the gospel as all Christians had at first received it, in the interests of their personal aggrandizement. St. Paul makes a brief but vigorous appeal to the Romans to be true to their first obedience, and maintain their reputation unsullied.

Now I beseech you, brethren, mark them which are causing the divisions and occasions of stumbling, contrary to the doctrine which ye learned: and turn away from them. For they that are such serve not our Lord Christ, but their own belly; and by their smooth and fair speech they beguile the hearts of the innocent. For your obedience is come abroad unto all men. I rejoice therefore over you: but I would have you wise unto that which is good, and simple unto that which is evil. And the God of peace shall bruise Satan under your feet shortly.

The grace of our Lord Jesus Christ be with you.

This abrupt insertion strongly reminds us of the Epistle to the Galatians (see i. 7-9, vi. 13), and of the similar outburst in the Epistle to the Philippians (iii. 1-3). St. Paul believed that such Judaizing teaching was inconsistent with the fundamental Christian 'tradition.' He does not imply that Rome was already corrupted, but he scents danger.

DIVISION VI. § 5. CHAPTER XVI. 21-23.

Salutations from St. Paul's companions.

Timothy my fellow-worker saluteth you; and Lucius and Jason and Sosipater, my kinsmen. I Tertius, who write the epistle, salute you in the Lord. Gaius my host, and of the whole church, saluteth you. Erastus the treasurer of the city saluteth you, and Quartus the brother.

Most of these persons are very probably otherwise known to us. Leaving aside the well-known Timothy, we find a Lucius of Cyrene among the prophets in Acts xiii. 1[1]; a Jason at Thessalonica, as St. Paul's host, in Acts xvii. 5 ff; a Sopater (or Sosipater) of Beroea, Acts xx. 4. Gaius was one of the few whom St. Paul had baptized at Corinth (1 Cor. i. 14), and the Christian church, it appears, met at his house. Erastus, the treasurer of Corinth, is probably the man mentioned in 2 Tim. iv. 20.

[1] And closely associated with St. Paul.

DIVISION VI. § 6. CHAPTER XVI. 25-27.

Final Doxology.

Now to him that is able to stablish you according to my gospel and the preaching of Jesus Christ, according to the revelation of the mystery which hath been kept in silence through times eternal, but now is manifested, and by the scriptures of the prophets, according to the commandment of the eternal God, is made known unto all the nations unto obedience of faith; to the only wise God, through Jesus Christ, to whom[1] be the glory for ever. Amen.

There is no idea in this doxology with which this epistle has not made us familiar in substance. We have been led to think of the gospel, now proclaimed and entrusted to St. Paul, as the disclosure of a divine purpose long working secretly: we have been bidden to adore the unfathomable resourcefulness of the wisdom of God: we have been constantly referred to the testimony borne by law and prophets to the gospels: we have been made familiar with the object of the evangelical preaching, as being to secure 'the obedience of faith among all the nations.' And a particular phrase in an epistle written about the same time[2]—'We speak the wisdom of God in a mystery, even the wisdom that hath been hidden, which God foreordained before the worlds unto our glory, which ... unto us God revealed by his Spirit,'—is strikingly parallel to the beginning of the doxology. At the same time the elaborate richness of the style, as well as many of the ideas, reminds us irresistibly of the Epistle to the Ephesians[3]. This, coupled with the fact that there is considerable authority for placing the doxology at the end of chap. xiv, has led some scholars to adopt the idea—accepted and elaborated by Dr. Lightfoot—that St. Paul first wrote the epistle down to xvi. 23, as his Epistle to the Romans, and subsequently, perhaps during one of his sojourns at Rome, turned it into a circular letter, omitting for this purpose the last two chapters, with their personal matter, and adding the doxology in the rich manner of the Epistle to the Ephesians. Subsequently the doxology would have been added also to the complete epistle. There are many difficulties in such a theory. Especially why should the beginning of chap. xv be cut off from the end of chap. xiv, when there is no break in thought? But I do not pursue the subject here[4], for it would be out of place, and alien to our practical purpose. There is no ground for doubting that the whole of what we receive as the epistle was written by St. Paul; and no ground for thinking that any part of the whole, down to xvi. 23, was not found in the letter as originally carried by Phoebe; but it cannot be denied that some mystery, not easily solved, hangs about the manifold and interrupted conclusions of the epistle; and that the rich style of the doxology is somewhat unlike both the rest of the epistle, and the other epistles of this period. However, whether or no it was written at a later date, at least it forms a splendid summing up of what is probably the greatest and most influential letter ever written.

And there is no teaching which we more urgently need to-day than the teaching of this epistle. Whether the need be to expand our personal religion into social service, and also to reinvigorate our social service with the power of personal religion; or so to reassert the divine authority of the Church as never to forget that it depends for its vitality upon personally converted hearts; or to teach men to remember the inexorable severity of divine judgement, as well as the depth of the divine compassion; or to rebuke the shallowness which attempts to separate Christian character from Christian doctrine; or to harmonize individual freedom with the social claim; or to impart to self-sacrifice the spirit of humility and gladness and indomitable hope; or at once to exalt and restrict the function of the State; or to emphasize the true grounds and limits of toleration in a catholic church—whatever, one may almost say, be the need to which the special deficiencies and perils of our church and age give rise, or of which at the moment we are most conscious, the teaching of St. Paul in this epistle is found to meet it full face.

Truly we may thank God with a continually growing gratitude for the gift to us of a letter so inexhaustibly full of spiritual wealth, and so complete in its provision for the whole of life.

[1] If we retain the words 'to whom' the grammar of the sentence breaks down, but the object to whom praise is ascribed is probably the Father.

[2] 1 Cor. ii. 7, 10.

[3] See especially Eph. iii. 1-13. Cf. also 2 Tim. i. 9-11; Titus i. 2, 3.

[4] It is fully treated in Lightfoot's Biblical Essays (Macmillan, 1894), pp. 287 ff, by Lightfoot himself and Hort from different points of view, and by S. and H., pp. lxxxv. ff.

APPENDED NOTES
NOTE A. See vol. i. p. 59.

THE MEANINGS OF THE WORD 'FAITH.'

The history of the original Hebrew and Greek words for believing or faith, is very interesting. The Hebrew verb ('aman') means 'to prop' or 'support'[1]. Now (1) a form of this verb means 'to be supported,' hence 'to be firm,' hence 'to be trustworthy'; (2) another form of the verb means 'to support oneself on,' and hence 'to trust,' 'to believe.' From (1) comes the Hebrew substantive ('emunah') meaning 'faithfulness,' 'trustworthiness,' which is used, as elsewhere, so also in Habakkuk ii. 4. In that passage it is revealed to the prophet, that, while the apparently overwhelming wave of Chaldaean barbarism rolls over him and passes away, 'the just man shall live (or save his life) by his faithfulness.' But this faithfulness of the righteous Israelite means a faithful holding on through the dark days to the word of God as to a secure ground of confidence; and thus the substantive used in this place in the Greek Bible ('pistis') tends to pass into the meaning which it mostly, though not always[2], has in the New Testament—a meaning derived not from form (1) but from form (2) of the Hebrew verb mentioned above (which however had no corresponding substantive)—trust or faith in the word and promise of another, especially God or Christ; or, still more characteristically, trust in the person of Christ and so of God.

Even under this heading of belief or trust the range of the word's meaning is considerable. In one passage of St. James' Epistle it is a bare intellectual recognition of the truth of things, without any moral value ('the devils also believe' that God is one, James ii. 19). More often it is that confidence in the divine word or promise, by which the good man, in lack of present evidence, sustains his courage or his prayer and wins his victory over the world: so especially in Hebr. xi, Luke xviii. 8, James ii. 23, 2 Cor. v. 7, 1 John v. 4. But its most characteristic use, as said above, is what first appears in the Gospels. The person of Jesus is there represented as eliciting from men a supreme trust in His power to heal diseases, and also to satisfy that deeper human need of which the disease is an outward symbol. And this power of Jesus to heal men in body and soul is seen in the Gospels to depend upon the extent of their faith: 'Thy faith hath saved thee;' 'According to thy faith be it unto thee.' Thus Jesus Christ appears constantly as inspiring, requiring, and rewarding faith in Himself, and that as the manifested Son of God, e.g. John xiv. 1. This is 'the faith which is through Him,' i.e. which He produces; and which as 'faith in His name' remains the characteristic Christian quality when He is gone from sight (Acts iii. 16). 'The faith' in the Acts (vi. 7, xiii. 8, xiv. 22, &c.) means this Christian attitude towards the unseen but living and energizing Christ.

Thus when St. Paul came to believe in Jesus Christ, 'faith in Jesus,'—as meaning not merely acceptance of His claim or of His word or of His grace, but whole-hearted devotion to His person, entire self-surrender or self-committal to Christ or God in Christ—became the dominant note of his new state: 'I know him whom I have believed, and I am persuaded that he is able to guard that which I have committed unto him against that day' (2 Tim. i. 12[3]). And this same devotion to Christ becomes, in St. Paul's theology, in its various stages, the only ground of man's acceptance with God. And though he uses 'faith' in a morally lower sense, as distinct from love—the faith which qualifies for miracles (1 Cor. xiii. 2)—yet in his characteristic sense of the term it involves the deepest love towards its divine object[4].

Naturally, as faith is thus the characteristic of Christianity, and this faith in a person involves a belief about Him—His divine sonship, His resurrection, His mission of the Spirit—so 'the faith' comes to mean (objectively) that which the Christian believes, or his creed; and this sense of the word appears almost in the Acts, in Gal. i. 23, and in Eph. iv. 5, and certainly in the Pastoral Epistles frequently (see Dr. Bernard in Camb. Gr. Test. on 1 Tim. i. 19) and St. Jude's Epistle, verse 2.

[1] We are familiar with the derived adverb of confirmation, 'Amen.'

[2] In Rom. iii. 3, Matt, xxiii. 23, it is still used for 'faithfulness.'

[3] In spite of Ellicott, Holtzmann, and Bernard, I believe this to be the true rendering, and not that of the R.V. margin.

[4] On the development of the principle of faith in the soul, see vol. i. pp. 29, 30; and on its naturalness, in the highest sense, for man, see pp. 21, 22.

NOTE B. SEE VOL. I. P. 103.

THE USE OF THE WORD 'CONSCIENCE.'

There is no word for conscience in the Old Testament. 'The conception,' says Delitzsch (Bibl. Psychology, Clark's trans., p. 160), 'is not yet impressed upon it.' And he accounts for this by quoting, 'The positive law took away its significance from the natural moral consciousness.' The Jews, that is—like other nations at certain stages of their history—lived so constantly under the detailed guidance of a law believed to be divine, that there was not much room for reflection as to the right and wrong of things. For the idea of conscience to develop, the will of God must be less clearly and decisively pronounced as to the details of conduct. There was, however, of course among the Jews, in proportion to their belief in a clear divine law, the consciousness of having done wrong; and on this account a man's 'heart' is described as 'privy to' an offence, and as 'reproaching' or 'smiting' him: see 1 Kings ii. 44, Job xxvii. 6[1], 1 Sam. xxiv. 5, xxv. 31, 2 Sam. xxiv. 10. Here is the root of the idea of conscience, i.e. of something in the man behind his surface self, reflecting upon what he has done, a self behind himself acquitting or condemning him, and so anticipating the divine judgement. For, as stated above[2], this was in the main the Stoic doctrine of conscience, and it was among them that the idea was first developed. Conscience was conceived of as that in man which lay behind his working self and reflected on his actions after they were done, bringing them into the light of the 'law of nature' or universal divine law for man. There is thus, as it were, in each man a double self, or double consciousness (conscientia), so that one can reflect upon himself, and pass judgement on his own actions.

It is in this sense of a self-judging faculty in all men reflecting on what they have done, anticipating a divine judgement, that the idea of conscience was acclimatized among the Jews. Thus, in Wisdom xvii. 11, we read, 'For wickedness, condemned by a witness within, is a coward thing, and being pressed hard by conscience, always forecasteth the worst lot.' In St. John viii. 9, according to one reading, the Jews are 'convicted by their own conscience.' So St. Paul, in the passage discussed above (ii. 15), seems to distinguish the subsequent reflective 'conscience' from the previous informing reason, 'the effect (equivalent) of the law written in their hearts.' And in most of the passages of the New Testament, this meaning of conscience—the faculty by which we sit in judgement on what we have already done—is sufficient. But sometimes, as also among the Stoics[3], the word passes into meaning the positive directing faculty, as when (1 Cor.

viii. 10) a man's 'conscience' is said to be 'emboldened' to adopt a new practice, or (Hebr. ix. 14) to be cleansed for positive service. Moreover, though it is an individual faculty (see Rom. ii. 15), and exists primarily to pass judgement on one's own actions only, yet perforce it must also look without and condemn or approve the actions of others (2 Cor. iv. 2, v. 11).

St. Paul also brings into notice that our conscience is a faculty for the condition of which we are responsible. It is not the voice of God, but a faculty capable of reflecting His voice, if it be well guarded. Thus you may have a 'weak' or a 'strong,' i.e. a more or less enlightened, conscience (1 Cor. viii). And a man may 'defile' his 'mind and conscience,' i.e. he may corrupt his moral reason and powers of moral self-judgement (Tit. i. 15). Then the 'conscience' may become hardened and 'seared' (1 Tim. iv. 2), so that 'the light that is in' men becomes itself 'darkness' according to our Lord's warning (St. Matt. vi. 23). And there is nothing which is more necessary at the present day than to remind men that they are not 'safe' because they are not acting against their conscience, unless they are also constantly at pains to enlighten their conscience and keep it in the light, by the help of the best moral thought of their time, the guidance of the Church and the word of God. Our conscience, if it is rightly to reassure us by its witness, must, like St. Paul's conscience, bear its witness 'in the Holy Ghost' (Rom. ix. 1).

With us moderns 'conscience' has generally the wider meaning of the whole practical moral consciousness. It enjoins as well as judges, and is occupied with the present and the future, as well as with the past.

[1] In LXX [Greek] ou gàr súnoida emautô átopa práxas.

[2] Vol. i. p. 103, n. 2.

[3] e.g. when conscience was described by Epictetus as the grown man's inward tutor [pedagogue], which must obviously mean that it is to instruct as well as reprove.

NOTE C. SEE VOL. I. P. 129.

RECENT REACTIONS FROM THE TEACHING ABOUT HELL.

There is no doubt that there has been within the last forty years a great, and in large measure legitimate, reaction from the old—mediaeval and Calvinist—teaching about hell. But one who reads the early chapters of the Epistle to the Romans, or the Gospels, or other parts of the New Testament, in view of this reaction, will probably feel an uncomfortable sense that it has gone too far. It is worth while then to try and discriminate.

To put the matter in as brief a summary as befits a note, I should hold that the reaction has been legitimate so far as it has involved a repudiation of—

(1) the Calvinist doctrine that God has created some men, no matter whether many or few, inevitably doomed to everlasting misery. This doctrine is flat contrary to some particular statements of the New Testament (as to its general spirit) and is only a misunderstanding of others (see above, pp. 8, 29).

(2) any such crude idea of the divine judgement as that God condemns men for merely external reasons, e.g. because in fact, apart from any question of will, they were not baptized, or remained pagans or heretics. Such a conception is quite inadequate, for the divine judgement penetrates to the heart. God is a father: He is absolutely equitable: He judges men in the light of their opportunities. He will reject none whose will is not set to evil. 'This is the judgement that ... men loved the darkness rather than the light, for their works were evil' (John iii. 19).

(3) the tendency to exaggerate what is revealed to us, and what, therefore, we can say we know about the state of man after death. Thus (a) there is nothing really revealed to us as to the relative proportions of saved and lost. (b) It is certain that we only know of a probation for man here and now— 'Now is the accepted time—now is the day of salvation.' And the absolutely equitable Father may see the conditions of an adequate probation equally in every man's earthly lot. It is therefore foolish to entertain, or encourage any one else to entertain, an expectation of any other state of probation except that which we certainly have here in this world. 'It is appointed unto men once to die, and after that the judgement.' But if St. Peter could speak (as of a familiar subject) of the 'gospel' as having been 'preached' by our Lord's human spirit in Hades 'to the dead,' i.e. to those who had perished in their wickedness under the divine judgement of the flood: and preached with the intention that the judgement might be turned into a blessing and means of spiritual life—and he certainly does speak thus (1 Peter iv. 6, cf. iii. 19): I do

not see how we can deny the possibility at any period, or in the case of any person, of an unfulfilled probation being accomplished beyond death. (c) Careful attention to the origin of the doctrine of the necessary immortality or indestructibility of each human soul, as stated for instance by Augustine and Aquinas[1], will probably convince us that it was no part of the original Christian message, or of really catholic doctrine[2]. It was rather a speculation of Platonism taking possession of the Church. And this consideration leaves open possibilities of the ultimate extinction of personal consciousness in the lost, which Augustinianism somewhat rudely, closed.

But to have convicted our forefathers of going, in certain parts of their teaching, beyond what was certainly revealed, affords no justification for doing the same ourselves in an opposite extreme; by asserting for example positively (a) that almost all men will be 'saved'; or (b) that there is probation to be looked for beyond death; or (c) that the souls of 'the lost' will be at the last extinguished. These positive positions are no more justified than those of our forefathers which we have deprecated. We must recognize the limits of positive knowledge.

And when we have come to the end of what a legitimate reaction from the teaching of our forefathers restores to us, in the direction of a 'larger hope,' we are still face to face with the fact of 'eternal judgement.' Men, as far as their individual destinies are concerned, are passing towards one of two ends, not towards one only—a divine judgement of approval or of condemnation; and both judgements are represented as final and irreversible; and they are the inevitable outcome of the moral law by which our probation is realized—that voluntary acts form habits, and habits stereotype into a fixed character. It is foolish to look to the process or moment of death for redemption from sin; for death, as far as we know, only transplants us with the character we have made for ourselves, and with continuous consciousness, into the unknown world; so that if in this life we have unfitted ourselves for God, we must find it out beyond death, and know there the full meaning of our awful miscalculation here. And the awakening of the 'lost' to what they have cast away—to the meaning of irreversible self-exclusion from the presence of God—is imaged as unspeakably awful; and their state is pictured in metaphors and phrases descriptive both of torment and finality—'outer darkness,' 'gnawing worm,' 'unquenchable fire,' 'eternal punishment,' 'eternal sin,' 'sin which shall not be forgiven, neither in this world, nor in that which is to come,' eternal 'death,' or exclusion from eternal life, 'eternal ruin,' 'wrath and indignation, tribulation and anguish.'

In face of all these sayings, it seems to me indisputable that 'universalism'— the teaching that there are to be none finally lost—is an instance of wilfulness. To speak of that which lies beyond death, even in the case of the worst and most impenitent criminal, as a place

'Where God unmakes but to remake the soul
He else made first in vain—which must not be,'

is, I cannot but feel, in flat contradiction to the whole tone of the New Testament.

It is no doubt true that there is in the New Testament an expectation of a final unity of the whole universe in God, and that we find it hard to conceive the relation of lost souls in hell to this final unity. Certainly all legitimate avenues of dim conjecture that a very limited revelation allows to be kept open, ought to be kept open. Certainly we know in part—the partialness of our knowledge can hardly be exaggerated. But we must be true to both elements in what is disclosed to us; and Dr. Martineau has reminded us[3] how deeply 'the belief in a separate heaven and hell, and a corresponding distribution of men into only two classes of good and bad, friends and enemies of God,' though 'at first sight nothing can appear more unnatural and defiant of all fact,' is yet bound up with 'the inward look' of moral evil and the fundamental reality of moral choice. In fact it seems to be true to say that a really Christian Theism, and a really Christian doctrine of human freedom, are inseparable from the belief in the possibility of wilful sin leading to final ruin.

'It is appointed unto men once to die, and after that the judgement'; and this judgement in the case of those of us who have wilfully hardened themselves, or remained loveless and love-rejecters, in face of the real offer of God to man in Christ Jesus, is a divine condemnation which takes effect in an eternal punishment, the bitterness as well as the justice of which the soul realizes, and which—if it does not necessarily mean an everlasting continuance of personal consciousness—is yet final and irreversible, and unspeakably awful[4].

[1] Summa, pars. 1, qu. 75, art. 6, 'Respondeo dicendum, quod necesse est dicere, animam humanam, quam dicimus intellectivum principium, esse incorruptibilem.'

[2] See Dr. Agar Beet's Last Things (Hodder and Stoughton, 1898), pp. 194 ff, and Gladstone's Studies Subsidiary to Butler (Oxford, 1896), part ii. pp. 260 ff.

[3] See Types of Ethical Theory (Oxford, 1885), ii. pp. 60 ff.

[4] The only passage in the New Testament which strongly suggests an everlasting persistence of personal consciousness of pain, is Rev. xx. 10, 'Shall be tormented day and night for ever and ever.' This is explicit

enough. But I am persuaded that all the numbers and expressions for periods of time in the Apocalypse are strictly symbolical. 'A thousand years,' 'forty and two months,' 'three days and a half,' 'day and night for ever and ever,' are expressions which have to be translated into some moral equivalent before they can be made the basis of literal teaching. Thus 'day and night for ever and ever' describes in a picture the completeness of the final overthrow and the anguish of the enemies of the Lamb. The symbolical character of the expression is further indicated by 'the beast' and 'the false prophet'—themselves symbolical figures—being with the devil the subjects of the torment.

Some will say that the deterrent effect of the doctrine of hell depends upon its being held to be a state of strictly endless conscious torment. I do not believe this is the case. The language of the New Testament is full enough of deterrent horror if we are faithful to it.

NOTE D. SEE VOL. I. PP. 143 FF.

DIFFICULTIES ABOUT THE DOCTRINE OF THE ATONEMENT.

I have endeavoured above to sketch the positive conception of the Atonement, as St. Paul seems to put it before us. Christ inaugurates the church of the new covenant, the new life of union with God. He lays its basis in a great act of reparation to the righteousness of God, which 'the old Adam' had continually outraged. This act of reparation lies in a moral sacrifice of obedience, carried to the extreme point by the shedding of His blood. This is the great propitiation in virtue of which God is enabled, without moral misunderstanding, to forgive freely the sins of any one who comes in faith to unite himself to Christ, and set him free to begin the new life.

The subject is a divine 'mystery,' and we shall never adequately probe it. Nay more, one man's thought will rightly seem inadequate to another, who has gained, or thinks he has gained, some special avenue of insight into the divine depths. But when we pass from special points of view, which are necessarily more or less individual, and can never become certainties for men in general—when we pass on to the ground of what should be the common church belief, the statement of the original revelation, it is not, it seems to me, liable to any of the familiar moral objections, or indeed a subject of any special difficulty. The difficulties experienced by the moral consciousness of our age have been due to gross and unnecessary misunderstandings, of which the following are, perhaps, the most considerable.

(1) The propitiation has become separated from the new life, for which it merely prepares the way. It has been elevated, with disastrous moral results, from a means to an end. Christ's work for us has been treated apart from His work in us, in which alone it is realized. He alone can act for all men, because He only can be their new life within. But on this see vol. i. pp. 141 f, and Ephes. pp. 54 ff.

(2) The idea of injustice has been introduced into the 'transaction' of the Atonement, and has been the most fruitful source of difficulty;—but quite unnecessarily. There is a story that when Edward VI was a child, and deserved punishment, another boy was taken and whipped in his place. This monstrously unjust transaction has been taken by Christian teachers as an illustration of the Atonement; and it is truly an illustration of the Atonement as they misconceived it. But the misconception is gratuitous:

there is no real resemblance in the two cases. For first, what is represented to us in the New Testament is not that Jesus Christ, an innocent person, was punished, without reference to His own will, by a God who thus showed Himself indifferent as to whom He punished so long as some one suffered. But He, being Himself very God, the Son of the Father, the administrator of the moral law and judge of the world, of His own will became man, and suffered what the sin of the world laid upon Him, in order that He might lift the world out of sin. Voluntary self-sacrifice for others is at least not to be described as injustice. At least we rejoice to recognize that God accepts such self-sacrifice. It is to vicarious self-sacrifice like our Lord's that the human race owes the greater part of whatever moral progress it has hitherto made.

Secondly, God is not represented as imposing any specially devised punishment on His only Son in our nature. As the matter is stated in the New Testament, He required of Him obedience, the obedience proper to man; and, if we regard sympathy with our fellow men as a part of our duty to God, we may say obedience only. Thus, 'Lo, I come to do thy will, O God' is the one cry of the Christ. In His simple acceptance of the whole of human duty lies the moral essence and value of His sacrifice. All the physical and mental sufferings of Christ came out of His fulfilment of the human ideal, Godward and manward, and were involved in it. He died because obedience to the terms of His mission—'the word of truth, and meekness, and righteousness'—in a world of sin such as this is, involved dying. 'He was obedient' without reserve—'unto death, even the death of the cross[1].' The value of the bloodshedding lies in this, so far as Scripture enables us to judge—that it represents utter obedience under conditions which human sin, the sin of Jews and Gentiles, laid upon Him: and it was in this sense, which does not leave out of consideration the mental torment caused to His sinless spirit by contact with sin[2], that He 'bare our sins in his body on the tree,' and that 'the Lord made to light on him the iniquity of us all.' What is ascribed to the Father is that He 'spared not' His only Son by miraculously exempting Him from the consequences of His mission; and that He foresaw, overruled, and used for His own wise and loving purposes the sin of men[3].

Thirdly and lastly, the Christ (as represented in the New Testament) did not suffer in order that we might be let off the punishment for our own sins, but in order to bring us to God. 'By his stripes we are'—not excused punishment, but—'healed.' In fact, there are two distinguishable punishments for sin. There is the spiritual punishment, which is involved in being morally alienated from God, which may become irreversible and eternal, but which is gone when the moral alienation is gone. From this Christ delivers us in making us at one again with the Father, but He

Himself did not endure it. God forbid that we should imagine such a thing! Besides this there is the temporal penalty which our sins bring as inevitable consequences upon ourselves and upon the race. All these consequences of human sin the sinless Christ bore for us, but not that we might be let off bearing them. We must bear them too—both the death of the body and the chastisement of particular sins. Christ bore the punishment of sins that were not His own, in order that in our case the punishments of sins which are our own might, through His bringing us back to God, be converted into healing chastisements and gracious penances. The record of God's dealings with His saints is still, as in Ps. xcix. 8, that they are heard, forgiven and punished.

How gratuitously then the idea of injustice has been introduced into the doctrine of Christ's sacrifice for us becomes evident when once it is brought within the scriptural limits. Christ suffered voluntarily. He suffered simply what was involved in becoming man in a world of sin. He suffered, the righteous for the unrighteous, that He might bring us back to God, that so we might have grace to bear our own sufferings and share His.

This alone, it seems to me, is what the New Testament certainly teaches. And the matter of most importance is that, ridding our minds of distracting and often needless difficulties, we should drink in, with heart and intelligence alike, the full force of what is certainly part of the Gospel—the doctrine of the one, full, perfect, and sufficient atonement with the Father, won for us by the self-sacrifice of the Christ.

[1] Phil. ii. 8; Hebr. x. 5-9.

[2] The perfect Man perfectly realized the misery and horror of the sins on behalf of which He suffered. How much is involved in this in the way of detailed realization of each individual sin of each individual sinner, is a matter on which we have no clear grounds for exact statement.

[3] I believe that nothing more than this is really suggested by Scripture. The phrase, 'made sin for us' (2 Cor. v. 21), means, I believe, according to the clear use of the word in the LXX, 'made a sin-offering for us.' The same words in the Hebrew stand for sin and sin-offering, and the use of the Greek follows: see especially (in LXX) Lev. iv. 31, 'It is the sin (= sin-offering) of the assembly;' 24, 'It (the goat) is a sin;' 29, 'He shall lay his hand upon the head of the sin;' vi. 25, 'This is the law of the sin'; viii. 14, 'The bullock of the sin.' Cf. Hos. iv. 8, &c.

NOTE E. SEE VOL. I. P. 196.

EVOLUTION AND THE CHRISTIAN DOCTRINE OF THE FALL.

There is a wide-spread and popular notion that a marked contradiction exists between the biological theory of evolution and the Christian doctrine of the Fall, which may be stated and examined under several heads:—

I.—'According to the theory of evolution man began his career at the bottom, emerging from purely animal life, and slowly struggled upwards to his present level of attainment. According to the Christian doctrine, on the contrary, he was created perfect, and then subsequently fell into sin and accompanying misery. Thus, according to one theory, man began at the bottom; according to the other, he began at the top.'

Now there is no doubt that when so stated the evidence is all in favour of the scientific point of view, and against the Christian. But such a contrast requires the greatest modification on both sides before it can be taken as truly representing the facts. Thus, it is not the case that the Bible suggests that man was created perfect, i.e. perfectly developed, and that his later course has been simply the effect of the Fall, i.e. a downward course. Leaving first out of account Gen. i-iii, we notice that the Bible is conspicuously, and in marked contrast to the religious books of other nations, the book of development. It looks continuously and systematically forward, not backward, for the perfecting of man. It traces the beginning of civilization in Abel, the keeper of sheep, Cain, the tiller of the ground, in Jabal, 'the father of such as dwell in tents and have cattle,' in Jubal, the father of music, 'of all such as handle the harp and pipe,' in Tubal Cain, the first forger of brass and iron work; it indicates the origin of religious worship (in some sense) at the time of Enoch, and the origin of building with the tower of Babel. The names of Noah, Abraham, Moses, Samuel, David, &c., represent stages of advance along the line of a chosen people; and later on it appears also that upon the chosen people centres a hope for all nations, and a purpose is discovered in universal history. The special intellectual qualities of various races or civilizations, as of Egypt and Tyre, are recognized by some of the prophets, and recognized as part of a divine purpose for the world[1]. The Bible then is the book of development; it looks forward, not backward. But it is also true that all this development is represented as having been (we may say) a second-best thing. It has not been according to God's first purpose. There has been a great and continual hindrance, which has consisted in a persistent rebellion or sin on man's part against God; and this again has had its root in a certain perversion of the heart of mankind which is regarded as approximately universal. If we now take into account again the first three chapters of Genesis (which, however, have left much less trace than is commonly supposed in the Old Testament as a whole[2]) we find that they describe an original act of rebellion on the part of the first human pair, which is there spoken of as at least entailing external consequences of a penal sort upon their descendants—that is death, pain, and the loss of Paradise; and that later, especially in the teaching of St. Paul, the universal moral flaw in human nature (original sin) is also represented as having its source in this initial act of rebellion.

Sin is therefore, according to our Christian scriptures, something unnatural to man: the violation of his nature by his rebellion; and it is a continual element of deterioration. But the idea that man was created perfect, i.e. so as not to need development, is not suggested. No doubt theologians, from the age of Augustine down to recent times, have done something more than suggest it. Thus Robert South supposes that 'an Aristotle was but the rubbish of an Adam, and Athens but the rudiments of Paradise'; and Milton implanted the idea in the imagination of Englishmen; but it is in no way suggested by the Bible, and was expressly repudiated by the earliest Christian theologians in east and west. Thus, in answer to the question whether Adam was formed perfect or imperfect, Clement of Alexandria replied, 'They shall learn from us that he was not perfect in respect of his creation, but in a fit condition to receive virtue.' And Irenaeus says that it was in the power of God to make men perfect from the beginning, but that such an initial perfection would be contrary to the law of human nature, which is the law of gradual growth[3]. We must therefore modify the statement of Christian doctrine from which we started, thus:—Man has been slowly led, or has slowly developed, towards the divine ideal of his Creator; but his actual development has been much less rapid and constant than it might have been, owing to the fact of sin from which he might have been free.

Now, can it be fairly said that science can take any legitimate exception to such a statement? The progress of man which anthropological science discloses is very broken, very partial; if development of some sort is universal, progress is very rare, distinct deterioration not uncommon. Science, like poetry and philosophy, must bear witness to the disappointing element in human nature, of which He was so conscious of whom it is said that 'He did not trust himself to man, because he needed not that any one should bear witness concerning man, for he himself knew what was in man'—the sad secret of human untrustworthiness and unsatisfactoriness[4].

Again, can science assert that this actual development of man, so thwarted and tainted and partial, has been the only possible development, and that there could not have been a better? If it cannot say this, there is in the general view of human progress and deterioration no antagonism between religion and science.

II.—But it may be said, 'Science certainly does say that the actual development of man has been the only possible development. Science excludes the idea of sin in the sense of something which need not have happened, because it excludes the idea of freedom or contingency altogether. Good and bad characters are like good and bad apples—mere facts of natural growth'; or more suggestively, 'Sin (so called) is only the survival of brute instincts, which, from a higher condition of evolution, men have come to be ashamed of.'

It cannot be made too emphatic that here is the real battle-ground of religion and science to-day, though the fact is often concealed in popular controversy. I do not believe there is any real difficulty in adjusting sufficiently the relations of religion and science as to the Fall when once the idea of sin has been admitted—that is, the idea of free, responsible action, with its correlative, the possibility of wrong action which might have been avoided. Christian and other teachers have, no doubt, often failed to see how limited human freedom is, but they have never been wrong in asserting that the reality of freedom within limits is essential to Christianity and morality. Sin is not a mere fact of nature. It is a perversion which ought not to have been. This subject is not what is directly before us now; but the heart of the controversy is here; and I will make the following very brief remarks upon it.

(1) A theory that cannot be put into practice, or a theory that cannot account for the facts, is a false or at least inadequate theory. Now the theory of necessary determinism cannot be put into practice. To believe that our own conduct is not really under our own control—that the idea of responsibility is at bottom an illusion—is to destroy the basis of human life and education. Even the holders of the theory admit that it must be kept out of sight in practice.

Further, it is a theory that cannot account for the facts—viz. for the existence of the universal sense of responsibility; and the application to human action of moral blame and praise, which penetrates the whole of thought and language, and which holds too large a place in human life to be a delusion. We are not ashamed of a physical accident, but we are ashamed of telling a lie. And this difference is fundamental and based on reality.

(2) The Christian assumption may be stated as follows: granted that we cannot increase the sum of force which passes from external sources into our system, and passes out again in manifold forms of human action, yet within certain limits we can direct it for good or evil—i.e. the 'voluntary'

part of a man's action may be determined from below, so to speak, by purely animal motives, or by rational and spiritual motives. In the latter case, the action is of the proper human quality, and stamps a rational and spiritual character upon all that falls within its range. In the former case, it may be truly regarded as a survival of the physical instincts of animal progenitors, and no doubt it emerges as a part of the physical order of the world. But, considered as human action, it represents a lapse, a culpable subordination of the higher to the lower in our nature, a violation of the law proper to manhood[5]. This is the point. St. John says, 'All sin is lawlessness,' and (by the exact form of expression which he uses) he implies also that all lawlessness is sin. Here, and here only where voluntary action begins, do you see violation of law, and therefore, within limits, a disturbance of the divine order—something which ought to have been otherwise.

(3) The belief that the moral evil of our nature does not properly belong to our nature but is its violation, and that if once the will be set right it can be remedied, has been the secret of the moral strength of Christianity. Christianity has said to all men, However corrupted your nature, the corruption does not essentially belong to you. Give your wills to God, and, if slowly, yet surely, if not fully in this world, then beyond it, all can be set right. 'According to thy faith be it unto thee.' And the practical power of this appeal, shows its agreement with reality.

(4) On the other hand, it cannot be claimed that the theory is contrary to any real scientific knowledge; for biology confesses that it knows very little as to the actual methods by which force is redistributed in human action. It is contrary only to some large and unverifiable assumptions—assumptions which ignore the abstract character of biological psychology, as of other sciences.

Now granted this reality of free voluntary action, it will hardly be denied that history discloses to us a practically universal prevalence of sin[6], in the present and in the past; and we can hardly fail to perceive, lying behind actual sins, a tendency to sin—what Shelley calls 'the ineradicable taint of sin,' a perverse inclination inhering in the stock of our manhood, which is what theology calls original sin.

III.—But here a more modern objection occurs. Christianity assumes that this moral flaw or taint, weakness or grossness, in human nature is the outcome of actual transgressions, in other words that original sin is due to actual sin, whereas the tendency of recent biological science is to deny that acquired characters can be inherited, and therefore to deny that any acts of any man or men could have any effect on the congenital moral nature of their descendants; the taint or fault in human nature, must be a taint or fault in that original substance which what is called man derived from his pre-human ancestry. To this I reply:—This is no doubt the view which Professor Weismann has made more or less prevalent. The substance of heredity ('germ-plasm') is taken to be a substance per se, which has always occupied a special 'sphere' of its own, without any contact with that of 'somatoplasm' further than is required for its lodgement or nutrition; hence it can never be in any degree modified as to its hereditary qualities by use-inheritance. It has been absolutely continuous 'since the first origin of life.'

But this doctrine does not appear yet to have assumed a fixed form[7]; and in its extreme or absolute form it is highly disputable, and rejected by large sections of biologists. Professor Haeckel[8] declares contemptuously that he should feel it more reasonable to accept the Mosaic account of special creations! The late Mr. Romanes, after summing up the evidence on both sides without any contempt, decides: 'No one is thus far entitled to conclude against the possible transmission of acquired characters[9].' Again, 'that this substance of heredity is largely continuous and highly stable, I see many and cogent reasons for believing. But that this substance has been uninterruptedly continuous since the origin of life, or absolutely stable since the origin of sexual propagation, I see even more and better reasons for disbelieving[10].' And he remarks[11], 'I doubt not Weismann himself would be the first to allow that his theory of heredity encounters greater difficulties in the domain of ethics than in any other—unless indeed, it be that of religion.'

I ought to add, in view of the apparently improbable event of the doctrine of Weismann becoming in its absolute form the accepted doctrine of biologists, that of course it only concerns the material organism. No one who is not a materialist would deny the possibility of the character of the parent modifying at its very root that of the child, without even the smallest conceivable modification of the physical organism; because in the origination of a spiritual personality, and in the link which binds it to the antecedent personalities to which it owes its being, there is that which lies outside the purview of biological science. There may be an inheritance of sinful tendencies derived from sinful acts in the region of the spiritual personality, even if no physical transmission is possible.

However it be explained, it appears to be the case that Christianity is bound to maintain the position that in the region of moral character there is, in fact, a solidarity in humanity. We are bound together. Our acts, as they form our own character, do somehow or other, however slightly, modify the characters of our descendants for good or evil. And this modification of the tendencies of the race by the acts of individuals may have been more marked at the beginning than it is to-day.

On the other hand Christianity is not in any way interested in denying that man derives a physical heritage of habits and tendencies from a pre-human ancestry. All I imagine that Christianity is interested in affirming is this—that when the animal organism became the dwelling-place of the human spirit (so to speak) that human spirit might have taken one of two courses. It might have followed the path of the divine will; and in that case human development would have represented a steady and gradual spiritualizing of the animal nature reaching on towards perfection. It might have taken, on the other hand, and did in fact take (more or less), the line of wilful disobedience. And the moral effects of this wilfulness and disobedience from the beginning onwards have been felt from parent to son. So that the springs of human conduct have been weakened and perverted, and no man has started without some bias in the wrong direction which would not have been there if his ancestors for many generations had been true to God.

It is worth noticing in passing that 'original sin' is not a fixed quantity derived from one lapse of the original man, but is a moral weakness continually reinforced by every actual transgression, and, on the other hand, reduced in force by moral resistance and self-control. Individuals start at very different levels of depravity. Only it would appear that practically in no man but One is there any reason to believe the fundamental nature immaculate.

IV.—But it will be said 'You have not yet touched upon a big central contradiction between religion and science. According to the Christian doctrine mankind is derived from a single specifically human pair, made human by a special inspiration of the Divine Spirit. According to the theory of evolution, a certain species of apes under specially favourable conditions gradually advanced to become what might be called man, though of a very low type.' To this I am inclined to make reply thus: Christianity is really bound up with maintaining four positions—(1) the reality of moral freedom; (2) the fact of sin, properly so called as distinct from imperfection; (3) its practical universality, at least as an inherited tendency; and (4) the unity of the human race in such sense that the same postulates may be made with regard to all men, and the same capacity for moral redemption (more or less) assumed to be in them. Now, as regards the first three of these positions enough has been said already, and the last of them does not appear to be at present in dispute between science and religion. St. Paul says, 'God made of one' (or 'of one blood,' for this reading is possibly right) 'every nation of men' (Acts xvii. 26). And of one blood, if not of one individual, all men are, according to the present conclusions of biological science. A recent work on ethnology, by Mr. Keane (Cambridge Geographical Series), speaks thus:—'The hominidae are not separately evolved in an absolute sense—i.e. from so many different anthropoid precursors, but the present primary divisions are separately evolved from so many different pleistocene precursors, themselves evolved through a single pliocene prototype from a single anthropoid precursor[12].'

It does not seem to me, then, that Christianity is really bound up with anything more than the unity of the human race, which science also strongly asserts. But to pass from these positions, which may be regarded as certain, to something more conjectural (apart from any question of the literary character of Genesis iii), we may argue thus: Sin is a fact having the same character universally in human history, though the sense of sin has varied greatly, reaching back as far as human history extends. This would lead us to suppose that it goes back to the roots of the race. It suggests some original fall, some tainting of the race in its origin. I do not see, then, anything absurd or contrary to evidence in such a hypothesis as this.—The Divine Spirit is assumed to be at work in all the development of the world. The 'laws of nature' are but His methods. At a certain moment a new thing had emerged in the universe hitherto inorganic. It was the fact of life. It was new[13]. But it was in continuity with what had gone before. This principle of life had its great development, vegetable and animal. It had attained a form in certain anthropoid apes such as we are familiar with in men. Suppose then that the Divine Spirit breathes Himself, again in a new way, into one single pair or group of these anthropoid animals. There is lodged in them for the first time a germ of spiritual consciousness, continuous with animal intelligence, and yet distinct from it. From this pair or group humanity has its origin. If they and their offspring had been true to their spiritual capacities the animal nature would have been more rapidly spiritualized in motives and tendencies. Development—physical, moral, spiritual—would have been steady and glorious. Whereas there was a fall at the very root of our humanity; and the fall was repeated and reiterated and renewed, and the development of our manhood was tainted and spoiled. There was a lapse into approximately animal condition, which is dimly known to us as primitive savagery. So that the condition of savage man is a parody of what God intended man in his undeveloped stages to be, just as the condition of civilized man in London and Paris is a parody of what God intended developed man to come to. And there have been long and dreary epochs when men have seemed to lose almost all human ideals and divine aspirations; when, in St. Paul's phrase, they were 'alive without the law,' living a physical life unvisited by the remorse consequent upon any knowledge of better things. And there have been, on the other hand, epochs and special occasions of spiritual opportunity and spiritual restorations. And so, on the whole, side by side with the continually deteriorating effect of sin, has gone on the slow process of redemption, the undoing of the evil of sin and the realization of the divine purpose for man. Such an idea of human history, partly only hypothetical, partly assured, conflicts with no scientific ethnology, and is but a restatement of old-fashioned Christianity in all that has religious importance.

V.—Of course, in all this I am assuming that the doctrine of sin and of the Fall in its true importance has a much securer basis than the supposition that Genesis iii is literal history. The doctrine of the Fall is, as I have said, not separable from the doctrine of sin, or the doctrine of sin from that of moral freedom. It rests upon the broad basis of human experience, especially upon Christian experience, which is bound up with its reality. Most of all it rests, for Christians, on the teaching of Christ. For Christ's teaching and action postulate throughout the doctrine of sin. But that doctrine in its turn goes back upon the Old Testament, which is full of the truth that the evils of human nature are due, not to its essential constitution, but to man's wilfulness and its results; that the disordering force in human nature has been moral, the force of sin; that human history represents in one aspect a fall from a divine purpose, a fall constantly reiterated and renewed in acts of disobedience. These constant acts of disobedience are in part caused by an evil heart in human nature, and this in its turn exhibits the fruits of past sins. Granted this, the story in Genesis iii, whether it be historical or whether (as not only many modern Christians, but some of the greatest of early Christians, have thought) it be not an historical account of a single event, but a generalized account of what is continually happening, has, at any rate, vital spiritual truth. The character of its inspiration is apparent. Teach a child what sin is, first of all on the ground of general Christian experience and the teaching of Christ, and then read to it the story of Genesis iii, and the child must perforce recognize the truth in a form in which it cannot be forgotten. There in that story all the main points of truth as to the meaning of sin are suggested, and the main sources of error precluded. Sin is not our nature, but wilfulness; sin is disobedience to the divine law, the refusal of trust in God; there is such a thing as being tempted to sin, and yielding to it, and then finding that we have been deceived, being conscience-stricken and fearing to face God; and the curse of our manhood springs from nowhere ultimately but our own evil heart. And if our sins lay us under an outward discipline, which is God's punishment, yet in the very discipline lies the hope of our recovery. God the destroyer is also the God who promises redemption. Thus all that we most need to know about God and man, about obedience and disobedience, about temptation, about the blessing and the cursing of human nature, about conscience good and bad, is to be found in the story of Genesis iii, written in language suitable to the childhood of the individual and of the race.

VI.—But once more, and for the last time, the biologist will reply, 'You are not going to get off so easily. The fact of physical death is inextricably interwoven into the structural growth of the world long before men appeared. But Christianity regards it as a mere consequence of human sin.' This is not the case. Long before science had investigated the early history of life on our globe, Christian teachers both in East and in West—St. Augustine as well as St. Athanasius—had taught that death is the law of physical nature, that it had been in the world before man, and that 'man was by nature mortal,' because, as being animal, he was subject to death. How, then, do they interpret the language of Scripture? In this way: They hold that if man had been true to his spiritual nature, the supernatural life, the life in God, would have blunted the forces of corruption, and lifted him into a higher and immortal state.

Certainly, in some sense, death, as we know it, for man, is regarded, especially in the New Testament, as the penalty of sin. But then what do we mean by death? If sin is said to have introduced human death, Christ is constantly said to have abolished it. 'This is the bread that cometh down from heaven, that a man may eat thereof and not die.' 'Whosoever believeth on me shall never die.' 'Christ Jesus abolished death.' Sin, then, we may suppose, only introduced death in some sense such as that in which Christ abolished it. Christ has not abolished the physical transition from this world to the invisible world, but He has robbed it of its terror, its sting, its misery. Apart from sin we may suppose man would not have died; that is, he would never have had that horrible experience which he has called death. There would have been only some transition full of a glorious hope from one state of being to another.

We are again in the region of conjecture. All that I am here interested in asserting is that Christianity never has held to the position that human sin first introduced death into the world. What it has taught is that human death, as men have known it, with its horror and its misery, has represented not God's intention for man, but the curse of sin.

VII.—Now I have endeavoured to face and meet the points which are urged in the name of science against the Christian doctrine of the Fall. I have endeavoured to point out that what is essential to Christianity is to believe in the reality of moral freedom, and the consequent reality of sin, as something which need not have been in the individual, or in the race considered as a unity. This is all that Christianity is really pledged to maintain. In maintaining this we are maintaining what is absolutely essential to the moral well-being of the race, and, moreover, what has the deepest roots in man's moral experience and in the teaching of Christ. In holding this we hold the doctrine of the Fall, a doctrine, that is, that man's condition has been throughout a parody of the divine intention, owing to the fact of sin tainting and spoiling his development from the root. But Christianity is not in any kind of way pledged against the doctrine of development, only against the doctrine which no reasonable science can hold, that the actual development of man has been the best or only possible one. Nor, I have urged, can it be reasonably said that the Christian doctrine of sin and of the Fall is bound up with one particular interpretation of Genesis iii. All, then, that we must admit in the way of collision between Christianity and science is, on the one hand, that Christianity is not intended to teach men science, and that when there is any great advance in human knowledge it takes a little while for Christianity to extricate itself from the meshes of the language and ideas belonging to one stage of scientific knowledge, and to assimilate the terms and ideas of the new. But, on the other hand, there is perennial and necessary warfare between Christianity and materialistic science, or a science which denies the reality of moral freedom. And as to Christianity giving up what is proper to its own ground—its teaching about freedom and sin and the Fall, and God's purpose for man, and the love shown in his redemption—to give up this is to give up what is the best and deepest motive of human progress, and what is most surely certificated by the witness of Christ and the spiritual experience of Christendom. Indeed all schemes of human improvement are shallow and inadequate, which do not deal with man as what, in fact, he has been proved to be, a sinful, that is a fallen, being, needing not only education but redemption.

Before leaving this attempt to show that there is no necessary conflict between biological and theological science, it is important to call the attention of the intelligent public to the fact that what formerly appeared to be the solid consistency of the 'Darwinian' creed, has been broken up into a state not far removed from chaos. It has become apparent how very little way has really been made towards showing what have been the actual factors in evolution—how the fact of evolution through variation has actually occurred. Thus Mr. Bateson[14] remarks, 'If the study of variation can serve no other end, it may make us remember that the complexity of the problem of specific difference is hardly less now than it was when Darwin first showed that natural history is a problem, and no vain riddle.' What is the cause of variations occurring? What law do they exhibit in their occurrence? Do variations occur with a certain degree of sudden completeness[15]? Or how are we to explain the maintenance of variations, which in a more developed stage are to be very useful, before they can be shown to be useful at all? What is the place held in evolution by 'natural selection'? What, if any, the place held by use-inheritance? Is the factor of 'mimicry,' supported by Darwin, an important or even real factor in evolution? What is to be the issue of the controversy between the biologist and the physicist on the question of the time required for organic development? Are we to suppose that organic development at the beginning proceeded very much more rapidly than at a later stage? Or even that it exhibited laws of which we have no experience now, such as would admit of a 'natural' development of life out of what is not living? All these, and many more questions, appear to be so completely open that, granted the general theory of continuous evolution as against special creation, hardly anything as regards the factors or causes of evolution can be said to be scientifically settled. Thus on such subjects as the origin of the human race, its exact relation to an animal ancestry, and the right interpretation of the fact of sin, before science can make demands on theology, there must be more agreement in her own camp.

[1] See especially Ezekiel xxviii, xxxi.

[2] See vol. i. p. 193.

[3] Clem. Alex. Strom, vi. 12. 96; Iren. c. Haer. iv. 38.

[4] See also above, vol. i. pp. 78, 79.

[5] On the meaning of 'freedom of will,' see vol. i. pp. 230 ff.

[6] See above, vol. i. pp. 80-1.

[7] Romanes, Examination of Weismannism (Longmans, 1893), pp. 61-70, 153.

[8] The Last Link (Black, 1899), p. 79.

[9] Romanes, Darwin and after Darwin (Longmans, 1895), ii. p. 279.

[10] Examination of Weismannism, pp. 114, 115.

[11] Darwin and after Darwin, ii. p. 90.

[12] See also in Haeckel, Last Link, p. 148: 'We assume the single monophyletic origin of mankind at one place, in one district'; and passages cited above, vol. i. p. 196, n. 1. The science of comparative religions also suggests the same conclusion. Everywhere common underlying religious needs and tendencies appear. Acts xvii. 27 is justified by a comparison of religions.

[13] It must not be left out of sight that the idea of life as naturally derived from what was inorganic, has not yet been made to appear even scientifically probable, in view of the evidence.

[14] W. Bateson, Materials for the Study of Variations, treated with especial regard to discontinuity in the origin of species (Macmillan, 1894), p. xii.

[15] Biologists are now apparently more disposed than formerly to admit the sudden appearance of considerable and important modifications and rapid developments. Cf. Haeckel, l. c. p. 144, and Bateson, p. 568. He concludes that 'discontinuity of species results from discontinuity of

variation.' 'The existence,' he says, 'of sudden and discontinuous variation, the existence, that is to say, of new forms having from their first beginning more or less of the kind of perfection which we associate with normality, is a fact that disposes, once and for all, of the attempt to interpret all perfection and definiteness of form as the work of selection. The study of variation leads us into the presence of whole classes of phenomena that are plainly incapable of such interpretation.' This relative perfection of variations at starting Mr. Bateson attributes in great measure to the principle of 'symmetry,' or 'repetition of parts' in living things. An organism is symmetrical, and thus what happens in one of many similar organs repeats itself normally in all the others. Change in one part is not an isolated fact, but there is 'similarity and simultaneity of change.'

NOTE F. SEE VOL. I. P. 215.

BAPTISM BY IMMERSION AND BY AFFUSION.

The following passage in the Didache, c. 7, is of the plainest importance for the history of this matter: 'If thou have not living [i.e. running] water, baptize into other water; and if thou canst not in cold, then in warm. And if thou have not either [in sufficient amount for baptism, i.e. immersion in the water] pour forth water thrice upon the head into the name of Father and Son and Holy Ghost.' Cf. Dr. Taylor, Teaching of the Twelve Apostles (Cambridge, 1886), p. 52: 'The primitive mode of baptism was by immersion. According to the Jewish rite a ring on the finger, a band confining the hair, or anything that in the least degree broke the continuity of contact with the water, was held to invalidate the act. The Greek word "baptize," like the Hebrew tabol, means to dip: to "baptize" a ship is to sink it. The construction [in the above passage of the Didache] "baptize into other water," points to immersion, as likewise does Hermas, when he writes (Simil. 9): "They go down therefore into the water dead, and come up living;" and Barnabas (chap. xi): "Herein he saith that we go down into the water laden with sins and filthiness, and come up bearing fruit in our heart, and having our fear and our hope towards Jesus in the Spirit." This was still the normal way of administering the rite, but it was no longer insisted upon as necessary: "If thou have not either," not enough of "living" or "other" water for immersion, "pour water thrice upon the head," &c.'

NOTE G. SEE VOL. II. P. 136.

A PRAYER OF JEREMY TAYLOR.

O holy and almighty God, Father of mercies, Father of our Lord Jesus Christ, the Son of Thy love and eternal mercies, I adore and praise and glorify Thy infinite and unspeakable love and wisdom; who hast sent Thy Son from the bosom of felicities to take upon Him our nature and our misery and our guilt, and hast made the Son of God to become the Son of Man, that we might become the sons of God and partakers of the divine nature; since Thou hast so exalted human nature be pleased also to sanctify my person, that by a conformity to the humility and laws and sufferings of my dearest Saviour I may be united to His Spirit, and be made all one with the most holy Jesus. Amen.

O holy and eternal Jesus, who didst pity mankind lying in his blood and sin and misery, and didst choose our sadnesses and sorrows that Thou mightest make us to partake of Thy felicities; Let Thine eyes pity me, Thy hands support me, Thy holy feet tread down all the difficulties in my way to heaven; let me dwell in Thy heart, be instructed with Thy wisdom, moved by Thy affections, choose with Thy will, and be clothed with Thy righteousness; that in the day of judgement I may be found having on Thy garments, sealed with Thy impression; and that, bearing upon every faculty and member the character of my elder Brother, I may not be cast out with strangers and unbelievers. Amen.

O holy and ever blessed Spirit, who didst overshadow the Holy Virgin-mother of our Lord, and caused her to conceive by a miraculous and mysterious manner; be pleased to overshadow my soul, and enlighten my spirit, that I may conceive the holy Jesus in my heart, and may bear Him in my mind, and may grow up to the fullness of the stature of Christ, to be a perfect man in Christ Jesus. Amen.

To God, the Father of our Lord Jesus Christ; to the eternal Son that was incarnate and born of a virgin; to the Spirit of the Father and the Son, be all honour and glory, worship and adoration, now and for ever. Amen.—Jeremy Taylor, Holy Living; see his Works, vol. iii. p. 238.

NOTE H. SEE VOL. II. P. 147.

THE ORIGIN OF THE MAXIM—'IN NECESSARIIS UNITAS, ETC.'

The expression 'In necessariis unitas, in non necessariis libertas, in omnibus caritas' is cited by Richard Baxter in the dedication of On the True and Only Way of Concord of all Christian Churches, 1679, thus, 'I once more quote you the pacificator's old and despised words.' But the pacificator appears to be no one older than a Protestant who wrote (1620 to 1640), under the name of Rupertus Meldenius, a Paraenesis votiva pro pace ecclesiae ad theologos Augustanae Confessionis. In the Paraenesis occurs the sentence 'si nos servaremus in necessariis unitatem, in non necessariis libertatem, in utrisque caritatem optimo certe loco essent res nostrae.' See A. P. Stanley in Macmillan, Sep., 1875, referring to G. C. F. Lücke, Ueber das Alter, den Verfasser, die ursprüngliche Fonn und den wahren Sinn des kirchlichen Friedensspruchs: 'in necessariis unitas &c.,' Göttingen, 1850.

This information was supplied me in correction of a mistaken attribution of the saying of which I was guilty in a sermon; and has been verified for me by Mr. Arthur Hirtzel. The saying has been commonly attributed to St. Augustine, and indeed the matter of it is thoroughly in his spirit; cf. my Ephesians, p. 272; and see also De Gen. ad litt., viii. 5: 'Melius est dubitare de occultis quam litigare de incertis.' De Civ. Dei, xix. 18: 'qua [i.e. faith in scripture] salva atque certa, de quibusdam rebus quas neque sensu, neque ratione percepimus, neque nobis per Scripturam canonicam claruerunt, nec per testes, quibus non credere absurdum est, in nostram notitiam pervenerunt, sine iusta reprehensione dubitamus.'

NOTE I. SEE VOL. II. P. 179.

ST. AUGUSTINE'S TEACHING THAT 'THE CHURCH IS THE BODY OF CHRIST OFFERED IN THE EUCHARIST.'

The following passages are full of interest:—De Civ. D. x. 6: 'So that the whole redeemed city, that is the congregation and society of the saints, is offered as a universal sacrifice to God by the High Priest, who offered nothing less than Himself in suffering for us, so that we might become the body of so glorious a head, according to that 'form of a servant' which He had taken. For it was this (our human nature) that He offered, in this that He was offered, because it is in respect of this that He is mediator, priest and sacrifice.' Then after a reference to Rom. xii. 1-6 he continues, 'This is the Christian sacrifice: the "many" become "one body in Christ." And it is this that the Church celebrates by means of the sacrament of the altar, familiar to the faithful, where it is shown to her that in what she offers she herself is offered.' And x. 20: Of Christ's perfect sacrifice of Himself 'He willed the Church's sacrifice to be a daily sacrament. For as she is the body of Him the head, she learns through Him to offer up herself.' Again xix. 23: 'God's most glorious and best sacrifice is we ourselves, that is His city, of which we celebrate the mystery in our oblations, which are known to the faithful.' Cf. xxii. 10: 'The sacrifice itself is the body of Christ, which is not offered to them (the martyrs), for they themselves also are it' (quia hoc sunt et ipsi). Cf. Serm. 227: 'If you have well received (the body of Christ in the sacrament) you are what you have received ... He willed us to be His sacrifice.'

In all this we have a very plain and much forgotten teaching. But we must not misunderstand St. Augustine's use of apparently exclusive language—as if the sacrifice of ourselves was the only sacrifice offered in the eucharist. The sacrifice of the Church is offered up through Christ. Thus he also speaks of the celebration of the eucharist (on the occasion of his mother's death, Conf. ix. 12) in the phrase 'the sacrifice of our ransom (pretii nostri) was offered for her.'

We do well to remember by the way that in De Civ. x. 5, 6, St. Augustine twice over defines what he means by sacrifice thus: 'A true sacrifice is everything that is done in order that we may by a holy fellowship inhere in God.'